SIX SIGMA
FOR PROJECT
MANAGERS

The books in the Project Management Essential Library series provide project managers with new skills and innovative approaches to the fundamentals of effectively managing projects.

Additional titles in the series include:

Managing Project Integration, Denis F. Cioffi

Managing Projects for Value, John C. Goodpasture

Effective Work Breakdown Structures, Gregory T. Haugan

Project Planning and Scheduling, Gregory T. Haugan

Managing Project Quality, Timothy J. Kloppenborg and Joseph A. Petrick

Project Leadership, Timothy J. Kloppenborg, Arthur Shriberg, and Jayashree Venkatraman

Project Measurement, Steve Neuendorf

Project Estimating and Cost Management, Parviz F. Rad

Project Risk Management, Paul S. Royer

MANAGEMENTCONCEPTS

www.managementconcepts.com

SIX SIGMA
FOR PROJECT
MANAGERS

Steve Neuendorf

MANAGEMENTCONCEPTS
Vienna, VA

(((
MANAGEMENTCONCEPTS

8230 Leesburg Pike, Suite 800
Vienna, VA 22182
(703) 790-9595
Fax: (703) 790-1371
www.managementconcepts.com

Printed in the United States of America

Library of Congress Cataloging-in-Publication Data

Neuendorf, Steve, 1951–
     Six sigma for project managers / Steve Neuendorf.
          p. cm. — (Project management essential library series)
     Includes index.
     ISBN 978-1-56726-146-2 (pbk.)
          1. Total quality management. 2. Six sigma (Quality control
     standard). 3. Project management. I. Title. II. Project management
     essential library.

HD62.15.N48 2004
658.4'04—dc22

                                                                    2004042628

About the Author

Steve Neuendorf has more than 25 years of consulting, management, industrial engineering, and measurement experience, including 15 years directly related to management, measurement, and improvement of software engineering projects and processes. Steve also has extensive management consulting experience. He has BA and MBA degrees from the University of Puget Sound with post-graduate work in information management, and a JD degree from Seattle University. Steve also has extensive teaching experience ranging from academics to hands-on workshops.

To Cristi and Kaylie with love

Table of Contents

Preface . . . . *xi*

CHAPTER **1** **What Is Six Sigma?** 1

CHAPTER **2** **Six Sigma As a Metric** 5
Defining Defects 6
Six Sigma As a Strategic-level Metric 8
Understanding Sigma-Level Metrics 10

CHAPTER **3** **Six Sigma As a Goal** 15
Improving Quality 15
Traditional Quality Control 16
Six Sigma Level of Quality 17

CHAPTER **4** **Six Sigma "by the Belts"** 21

CHAPTER **5** **Implementing a Formal
Six Sigma Program** 23
Focus on the Customer 24
Data- and Fact-driven Management 25
Process Focus on Management and Improvement 25
Proactive Management 27
Boundaryless Collaboration 28
Drive for Perfection, Tolerance for Failure 29
Successful Six Sigma Implementation 31

CHAPTER **6** **"Ultimate" Six Sigma** 35
Benefits of Ultimate Six Sigma 36
Additional Tools 42

CHAPTER **7** **Applying Six Sigma to
Project Management** 47
Process Issues 47
Measurement Issues 49

CHAPTER **8** **Organizing for Six Sigma** 61

Vision 61

Skills 63

Incentives 64

Resources 65

Action 65

Index 67

Preface

Writing a book about six sigma at first seemed like an easy and fun task. After all, I have been closely involved with the implementation of six sigma in a large company, back when six sigma was popularized by Motorola's success winning the first Malcolm Baldrige National Quality Award in 1988. My background in industrial engineering and measurement seemed like the perfect basis from which to elaborate on six sigma for project managers. I also was aware of several companies participating in what seemed to be a six sigma revival. My curiosity was piqued when I heard martial arts terminology applied in the context of six sigma, but some casual research left me with the impression that this was an isolated, esoteric approach that didn't really affect the foundations of six sigma.

Needless to say, when I started doing some research, I was in for quite a surprise about what had transpired in the six sigma arena. Writing a book about six sigma primarily for project managers clearly raised a dichotomy. My initial impression was that what I would have described as traditional project management is not employed in a comparable form in most of the six sigma efforts I found documented. The perennial debate over whether subject matter knowledge and experience are of greater importance than project management knowledge and skill is evidenced by a mix of both sets of qualifications in practice. In many forms of six sigma, a black belt is an absolute prerequisite for being a six sigma project manager. Of course, the implication is that a book on "Project Management for Black Belts" may be easier to focus than one where the audience does not have a reasonable expectation of being asked to manage a six sigma-related project without significant exposure to the principles of the six sigma method and the typical "internship" prerequisite for earning the black belt designation.

As I continued to research, I found that there are nearly as many versions of six sigma as there are practitioners. Six sigma is really a tool, so it truly can be applied in many variations; its effectiveness is determined far more by the skill of the user than by the tool itself.

The audience for this book is project managers, who probably have come to need to know more about six sigma because the organization they are working for is considering or is in the process of implementing six sigma. Perhaps these project managers are looking for a job and are considering employers who have implemented or are considering implementing six sigma.

Six sigma in its myriad variations is a collection of some really good ideas and tools that many organizations have used to significantly improve the quality of their products and services. Others, however, have failed miserably and ended up doing damage to themselves and their customers. As project managers, we understand the risks associated with change and with potentially dangerous tools. It's like using fire: we can warm our house or burn it down.

I have outlined two main variants of six sigma in this book in addition to discussing six sigma as a measure and as a goal. I have also included a chapter discussing the application of six sigma principles to project management. I hope you find this helpful.

Steve Neuendorf
March 2004

CHAPTER 1

What Is Six Sigma?

Sigma (σ) is the Greek symbol used in statistics to indicate the statistical property of a set of grouped data called "standard deviation." If you are fairly well versed in statistics, you would say that is pretty elementary; if not, you would say it's Greek to you. Either way you would be right.

"Grouped data" refers to any set of data that are somehow related. If you are rolling dice, for example, all the data from each roll for however many rolls would be grouped data, because all the data come from the same system of rolled dice. Eventually, after rolling the dice enough times and analyzing the results, you no longer need to roll the dice and collect and analyze the data to predict the likelihood of the next roll or several rolls. We would say that rolling a 7 is the most likely outcome, since there are several ways the dice can be rolled to give a 7, just as we can say that rolling a 2 or a 12 is the least likely outcome, since there is only one way to roll either of those results.

With some analysis, we could create a "probability distribution" for rolling the dice that showed the probability of rolling any particular result. Lots of statistics can be derived from this type of data, but the ones we are interested in are the standard deviation, σ, and the average or mean—that is, the most likely result.

For any given distribution, the percentage of the results that falls within 1 standard deviation of the mean is a constant. Further, the percentage of results that falls within any number of standard deviations is a constant. For a normal distribution, about 64% of the results will fall within 1 standard deviation of the mean (1σ), about 95% will fall within 2 standard deviations of the mean (2σ), and about 99.9% will fall within 3 standard deviations (3σ) (see Figure 1-1). For the mathematical derivation of six sigma, the area under the curve is 99.999999998%; in other words, about 2 parts per billion (ppb) are not under the curve. To illustrate, 2 ppb of the world's population (as of early 2003) would be 12 people.

While six sigma is at its roots all about statistics, in its application and practice it is very little about statistics except to a very few people. It is not

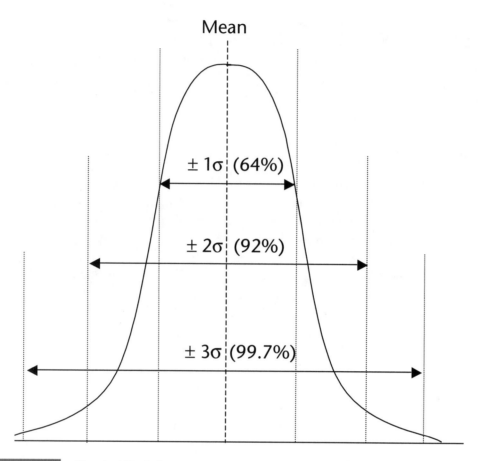

FIGURE 1-1 Standard Deviation

likely to have much, if anything, to do with statistics for project managers. By analogy, temperature is all about the average speed of molecules, but making the room warmer has more to do with starting a fire, turning up the thermostat, or shutting the window than it does with the molecules and how they are moving. In the analogy, the result—a warmer room—is what is important; in six sigma, improved quality is what is important.

Nevertheless, we should note that standard deviation is a property of the number set. Since we are attributing the results represented in the number set to the measured results of a process, we can say that standard deviation is a property of the process. Any process will also have its "design objectives" as defined by its creators. This property is the "spec limit" or the "performance standard" for that process.

If we look at a manufacturing process, the spec limit might be expressed as a range about a dimension, such as a length of $10'' \pm 0.1''$. If the process is returning a customer call, the spec limit or performance standard might be stated as "by the end of the next business day." No matter what it is, we can treat the specification limit as independent of the observed statistics (mean and standard deviation) for that process. If the process is designed so that the performance distribution falls well within the spec limit or performance standard, then we would say we have "good quality"—that is, very few defects as defined by comparing the results with the spec limit or performance standard. On the other hand, if the process is defined so that a lot of the results fall outside of the spec limit, then we would say we have poor quality in the results.

So what can we do?

Changing the spec would be effective, but tough to do in the world of interchangeable parts or the need to make a good customer first impression. Changing the results (i.e., fixing all the defects) would be effective but expensive and wasteful. Or we can change the process to make sure that the most probable outcome is a result within the specification limits. Remember, the "tighter" the process (i.e., the smaller the standard deviation), the higher the percentage of the results that falls within the specification limits or performance standards.

Six sigma, or any statistical process control tool for that matter, is really about developing a congruency between the specification limit (performance standard) and process performance, such that the process is designed to perform within the specification limit. Six sigma goes one step further in "normalizing" the measurement of quality for use in any type of process or activity.

Just in the examples we have used so far—the dice, the temperature, the length, and the call return—we have four different units of measure: integers, degrees, inches, and business day. To the people responsible for any of these processes, the units of measure have meaning and usefulness, but to someone with responsibility for all of these processes collectively, the measures would only confuse whatever information is needed to manage these disparate processes effectively.

What six sigma does at the result level is express measurement as "defects," which can be defined as any failure to meet the specification limit or performance standard, and opportunities for defects, which can be defined as any place where the measurement could have indicated that a defect occurred. Further, the quality level is usually expressed as "defects per million opportunities for defects" (DPMO), or more succinctly as ppm (parts per million). With any activity's quality performance expressed as defects per million opportunities, one can effectively compare performance between very different activities and make decisions about where and how to focus improvement activity and resources.

As noted, if we measure any process, the results will be a set of grouped data. If we are measuring the number of defects produced by our process, we quantitatively know how much the process produced and how many defects were contained in that process.

Processes are somewhat like the concept of inertia in physics, which is that an object will remain in a constant state until it is acted upon by an outside force. Processes will tend to reproduce the same results until they are acted upon by an outside force. So, if you have a process that tends to produce so many defects in some measured amount of its output, that process can be expected to continue to produce that same number of defects until someone does something to change it. Once the process is changed and it has a new characteristic for producing defects (or for producing defect-free output), it will continue to operate at that level until it is acted upon again.

Organizations tend to think that projects are the alternative to process. That is, if something is done routinely there is no need to initiate a project to get it done. If we need something done just once or done differently from what we have done in the past, we might charter a project.

CHAPTER 2

Six Sigma As a Metric

Measures are raw data; metrics comprise one or more measures expressed in a context that gives them meaning or usefulness that the measures by themselves may not have.[1]

Metrics can be grouped into categories according to what types of activities and decisions they tend to reflect and support. Figure 2-1 identifies the general categories of measurement. Interestingly, the six sigma metric DPMO can be considered in the efficiency measurement category, especially when we look at the efficiency of matching the defect removal rate to the defect introduction rate for products and services. Alternatively, it can be considered in the effectiveness measurement category, where eliminating the production of defects is considered the right thing to do.

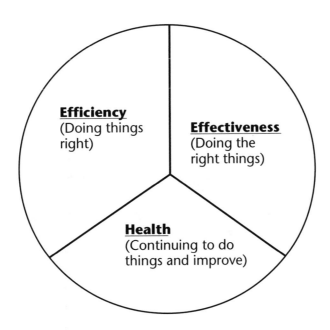

Efficiency
(Doing things right)

Effectiveness
(Doing the right things)

Health
(Continuing to do things and improve)

FIGURE 2-1   Categories of Measurement

DEFINING DEFECTS

At its roots, six sigma is a metric; that is, two measures are used to derive the sigma value for quality for any given product or process:

1. The number of defects in that product or within an execution of that process
2. The number of opportunities for defects within that product or within an execution of that process.

As shown in Figure 2-2, some of the opportunities for defects are realized as defects. Much like "realized" and "recognized" in taxes, they are evident as defects only if they are measured at the appropriate control points in or after the process; otherwise, they manifest themselves as failures in subsequent steps of the process or in the hands of the end customer.

This sounds simple enough, but rigor must be used in defining a defect. Once a defect is defined, it is fairly easy to identify the number of opportunities; again, one must be rigorous.

Major problems with quality and quality management often arise as a result of the lack of some common operating definitions of terms. Figure 2-3 shows the terms used throughout this book, and how they relate.

Figure 2-3 distinguishes between internal and external and between errors and defects, but we generally refer to them collectively as defects. In practice it will be necessary to make these defect classification distinctions to evaluate the effectiveness of improving process (i.e., eliminating faults) with the resultant reduction or elimination of errors. In essence, achieving six sigma is much more about discovering and eliminating faults, which would eliminate all types of defects and all types of failures associated with defects.

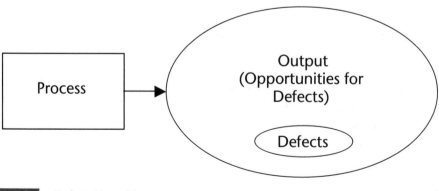

FIGURE 2-2   Defects Venn Diagram

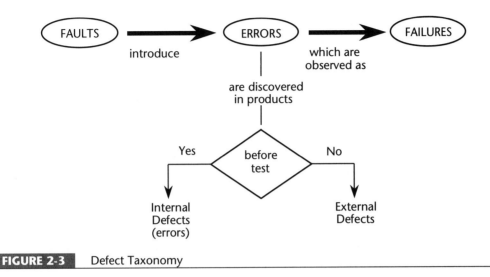

FIGURE 2-3   Defect Taxonomy

The quality of a product or process is expressed as its defect density. This defect density is then compared with a standard determination of the sigma level associated with that particular value of defect density. The lower the observed defect density, the higher the sigma level for the quality of that set of products or process results.

A defect is not a direct measure. For example, say a manufacturing process produces a part that is supposed to be a certain length. The length of parts is measured as they are produced. Although the measures vary, the parts that fall within the range of the specified length plus or minus an also-specified length tolerance range are deemed "good" while those parts where the measured length falls outside of the specification range are considered defects. Each part produced is an opportunity for a defect with respect to its length. The defect density is the number of defective parts with respect to length divided by the total number of parts produced (or opportunities for defects).

Length is not the only aspect of the part that has a specification associated with it. A requirement for width may also be associated with the piece. Just as with length, when one part falls outside the width specification, it is counted as a defect. Again, each piece produced represents an opportunity for a width defect.

Defects do not have to be associated with a quantitative measure. A subjective specification such as "free of scratches" may be verified by an optical inspection step in the process. Any piece that is scratched in a manner that it would be considered not to meet this requirement would be counted as a defect; each piece produced would be counted as an opportunity for this type of defect.

Thus, each part may have many opportunities for defects and each part may also have many defects. This should also raise the question of what to do in the case where a part that contains a defect is rejected. Is the rejected part checked for defects against the other possible opportunities? The process of determining the right defect density level for a particular product or process can be complicated and is a possible source of error. An erroneous measure of defect density can cause a problem to be overlooked or create a situation where something that is not a problem is "corrected."

It is also important to make the distinction between a defect and a failure. A computer crash, a customer complaint, and a car that won't start are all failures. The relationship between defects and failures is "zero one or many to zero one or many." That is, a failure can occur even if there are no defects. Conversely, a defect may not result in a failure. Moreover, many defects can cause a single failure and one defect can cause many failures. In the calculation of the defect density using six sigma conventions, the distinction between defects and failures is very important.

SIX SIGMA AS A STRATEGIC-LEVEL METRIC

The different levels of an organization's metrics program identify a minimum of three levels: a strategic level, a tactical level, and a technical or operational level.[2] Six sigma is a strategic-level metric. It can be used to express the quality of a product or of a process. More specifically, six sigma describes the characteristic of a process to produce defects or the results of a process (products) to contain defects. While it is possible to consider the quality of production or delivery of services an operational and tactical endeavor, six sigma treats it as a long-term strategic goal (see Figure 2-4).

To understand the usefulness of six sigma as a metric, it is necessary to understand that any process has certain properties or constants, including the cost required to execute the process (generally referred to as efficiency (E) or productivity), the quality of the results of the process (measured here as the defect density expressed in units of sigma (σ)), and the time it takes for that process to execute under defined conditions (referred to as the cycle-time (T)). It usually gets a smile when you tell someone "good, fast, or cheap—pick two," but this proposition reflects the nature and the interrelationship of these properties (dependent variables) for a process. The following expression

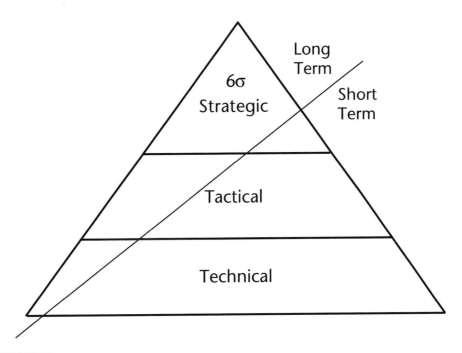

FIGURE 2-4   Metrics Program Structure

describes the general relationship between these parameters for any selected process:

$$f(E, \sigma, T) = K \quad \text{where K is a constant for that process.}$$

Defining "process" as a group of steps, methods, and means that are used to produce a result, it could be said that everything done is the result of a process. Certainly in business or in the endeavors of any organization, success depends on having the processes and executing them at the right level, time, and place.

Since every process has the property of quality, it is possible to apply six sigma measurement to evaluate the quality performance of that process. So, as a strategic metric, sigma quality metrics can be used to compare quality performance and performance improvement between departments or product lines using valid and accurate measures without the need to understand or interpret the differences between the underlying processes being evaluated and compared.

While sigma-level metrics work very well at the strategic level, they are not particularly well-suited for use as tactical or operational metrics. You would not get the desired result, for example, if you were to tell the operator of a machine that a higher level of sigma was needed in the next quarter. But if you focused the instruction on a particular type of defect and the operator was able to reduce the number of rejects for that type of defect without changing the rate of production for other types of defects, then the quality performance, as measured in sigma units, would improve.

By the same reasoning, sigma metrics use measures that are also used to produce other tactical and operational metrics that are more specifically focused on process control and decision points. If these other metrics are used to execute effective control and make the right decisions that improve processes, the later analysis evaluating the sigma level of the process and the effects of the changes should reflect the improvements. In and of themselves, however, the sigma metrics are only the quantitative assessment of performance and change, not insight into what constitutes quality or the nature of the changes.

It is as important that sigma quality measures evaluate the quality performance of a process as it is that they evaluate the changes in the quality performance for a process. As a strategic metric, sigma quality metrics are useful to an organization in evaluating efforts to improve the processes used to fulfill the organization's mission. So, sigma metrics can be unambiguously used to evaluate the performance and the change in performance between any processes employed by the organization and over any time period selected to evaluate the effectiveness of efforts to improve.

Six sigma is expressed and reported as the sigma level associated with the observed ratio of defects per opportunity for defects, or more specifically, defects per million opportunities. The sigma level of quality is generally expressed analogous to the chemical terminology of parts per million (ppm).

UNDERSTANDING SIGMA-LEVEL METRICS

A precise and detailed discussion of the statistical nature of sigma-level metrics is beyond the scope of this book, but a general description of the measures and metric we refer to as "six sigma" provides useful background for considering the application of six sigma to project management.

Sigma is a symbol (the Greek letter "σ") used in statistics to represent standard deviation. Standard deviation is a measure of dispersion for a related group of data that represents the result measure for the performance or output of a particular process. These results are distributed in some non-random fashion and statistics are used to describe the nature of that distribution. For example, the mean is the arithmetic average of the measured values, the median is the value at which there are an equal number of values below and above, and the mode is the most commonly occurring value.

Measures are generally taken at a point and in a way that the distribution conforms to some defined distribution, like the "normal distribution," for which certain statistics are well defined and understood. Standard deviation is a measure of dispersion and it is determined in such a way that a fixed percentage of the distributed values falls within a given number of standard deviations of the mean. For example, in statistical process control (SPC), the control limits for a process are at plus or minus 3 standard deviations of the mean. That is, for normally distributed values, 99.7% of the values fall within plus or minus 3 standard deviations, or $\pm 3\sigma$.

Anything that falls outside the control limits is said to be the result of a special cause of variation. Again considering the properties of a process, take the example of the length of a component. The engineers will specify a length and a tolerance, usually plus or minus an equal amount. The process that cuts the pieces to length will also have a mean length plus or minus some amount. If the machine that performs the cut-to-length operation is designed and controlled so that the tolerance limits set by the engineers correspond to the $\pm 3\sigma$ performance of the process, then 99.7% of parts will correspond to the length requirement. The more the process can be "tightened up" so that the tolerance corresponds more than $\pm 3\sigma$, the higher the percentage of parts produced that meet the length specifications. From a pure statistical perspective, the ppm defective for $\pm 3\sigma$ would be 27 parts per million, while the percentage defective for $\pm 6\sigma$ would be about 2 parts per billion.

Even though six sigma is applied in every type of process in every type of industry and organization, its roots are deep in manufacturing. Manufacturing is generally set up in "runs," so that a machine is set up for a run with sharp tools and its setting and adjustments at a certain value at the beginning of the run. As the machine vibrates and the tools dull, the output of the process tends to shift.

In our length example, the machine may be set up to cut on the short end of the tolerance range. As the cutter wears, dulls, and loses its set, the cut pieces tend to get longer and longer until the mean cut is at the longer end of the tolerance range. At some point in production, the machine is stopped, the cutter is replaced or sharpened and reset, and a new batch is initiated. To allow for this type of wear, the practical application of six sigma considers a mean shift of 1.5 standard deviations; the translation of defect density to sigma metrics is such that six sigma corresponds to a defect rate of 3.41 defects per million opportunities (DPMO).

Figure 2-5 illustrates the relationship between various levels of sigma metrics and defect densities.

Sigma Level	Defects/Million Opportunities (DPMO)
0	> 941,000
1	693,000
2	308,000
3	67,000
4	6,200
5	230
6	3

FIGURE 2-5   Relationship between Sigma Levels and Defect Densities

Mathematical Approximations for Six Sigma

The following formulas can be used to approximate the defect rate associated with a level of sigma or the sigma level associated with a defect rate. Note that these formulas have a mean shift of ± 1.5σ already included.

To approximate the defect rate in DPMO for a given sigma level S:

Fraction defective $P = \dfrac{DPMO}{1,000,000} = \left[a_1 t + a_2 t^2 + a_3 t^3\right]\left[\dfrac{1}{\sqrt{2\pi}} e^{-\left(0.5(S-1.5)^2\right)}\right]$

Where $t = \dfrac{1}{1+c(S-1.5)}$

and $c = .333$ $a_2 = -.120$
       $a_1 = .436$ $a_3 = .937$

To calculate the sigma level for a given DPMO:

Calculate the fraction defective $P = \dfrac{DPMO}{1,000,000}$

Sigma $(S) = t - \dfrac{a_0 + a_1 t}{1 + b_1 t + b_2 t^2} + 1.5$

Where $P < 0.94$ and $t = \sqrt{(-2\ln P)}$

and $a_0 = 2.308$ $b_1 = 0.992$
       $a_1 = .271$ $b_2 = .045$

Many decision makers shy away from six sigma because of the apparently complicated mathematics or the prevalence of examples showing how six sigma is applied in manufacturing or in highly repetitive processes. The math really just provides visibility for the overall progress and impact of the much more pragmatic quality and process improvement efforts. Most basic six sigma examples are from applications in repetitive manufacturing; that is where six sigma has its roots, and those are therefore the most illustrative examples of the principles.

There is also a considerable amount of more advanced literature describing applications of six sigma to custom work and to knowledge work. Think of the sigma metric as the mileage for a journey. Six sigma is the destination and you can review where you are starting from to determine how long the journey will be. You can check your position along the way to see how much of the journey remains and review how far you have come. Still, the focus is on the journey itself and the means, methods, and modes of travel, just as the focus of the six sigma journey is on the analysis and improvement of processes and consequently the improvement of quality.

NOTES

1. For an in-depth discussion of measures and metrics, see Steve Neuendorf, *Project Measurement* (Vienna, VA: Management Concepts, Inc., 2002). © 2002, Management Concepts, Inc.

2. Ibid.

CHAPTER 3

Six Sigma As a Goal

B roadly stated, the goal of any organization is to fulfill its mission. For a commercial organization, that may mean satisfying its owners by acquiring and satisfying customers and remaining viable. For a public organization, it may mean delivering services effectively with the level of resources allotted. Any type of organization can express its goals in terms of the relationships it has with those inside and outside the organization with whom it must interact and coexist. However these goals are characterized—as "vision," "mission," "goals," "objectives," or combinations of these terms with specific operating definitions—organizations have a reason to exist and a direction for the present and the future.

At a lower level, any organization's goals can be expressed as a performance level and almost always as an imperative to improve. For an organization to exist and continue, it must have some level of quality, responsiveness, and affordability. With rare exceptions, organizations must also continually improve to remain viable against competition and alternatives.

IMPROVING QUALITY

In this framework, a six sigma program is about improving processes to achieve better quality. We have loosely defined quality using the six sigma definition of defects per opportunity for defects. At the level of goals, quality also has to include other definitions such as: "conformance to specification," since all elements of conformance may not be defined as defects or opportunities; and "fitness for use," in that the products or services may be free of defects but not really what the customer needed.

Ultimately, quality must be whatever the customer says it is. So while "being six sigma" may be important to an organization, the customer would give that only scant consideration in evaluating the quality of the product or service. An old saying was that "unless you're the phone company, you don't have dissatisfied customers." Now even phone companies have to worry about satisfying—or otherwise losing—customers.

The sigma quality performance level of any process is a property of that process. That is, the value exists; all we need to do is measure it. A lot of activity taken to change a process will also change the sigma performance level for that process, even if we do not measure it or even understand what it is. There are few businesses—or few aspects of any business—that are not candidates for some level of improvement in performance, be it quality (better), cycle time (faster), or cost (cheaper). Tongue in cheek, we say "better-faster-cheaper—pick two," but the reality of improvement is that we must achieve some level of improvement in all three, which means we must change the process.

TRADITIONAL QUALITY CONTROL

Traditional quality control looks first at finding defects (i.e., discovery rate) and then fixing them (i.e., defect removal rate). Actual practice is more like letting the defects "find themselves," or evaluating the failure rate and then fixing the damage (failure consequences) and possibly also fixing that particular instance of the defect. The next step is often actually fixing the process to reduce the production of defects. In general, traditional quality control seeks a balance where the ability to detect and fix defects equals or exceeds slightly the propensity of the process to produce defects.

Figure 3-1 shows the relationship between the rate of addition of defects and the rate of removal of defects. The "cost of quality" (COQ) contribution for "detection" and "correction (and failure)" is also represented in each quadrant. The cost of quality contribution for "prevention" consists of the cost of defect prevention, detection, and correction.

The upper right and lower left quadrants clearly represent determinative states of the relationship between the rate of addition of defects and their removal. The upper right quadrant has a very high cost of quality while the lower left quadrant has a low cost of quality. The lower left quadrant clearly represents the state of the process being "in control." In considering this view of quality, include the "cost of prevention" or activity directed at reducing the rate of defect addition. Clearly, the cost of implementing a six sigma program would be in this category.

Consider that as quality approaches six sigma, the rate of defect addition becomes so low that the rate of detection and removal becomes inconsequential. Where you have achieved the perfection (or nearly so) of six sigma, the COQ becomes the cost of maintaining six sigma performance. In low sigma processes, experienced business and project managers should recognize that the COQ can account for a significant portion of the cost of any process or

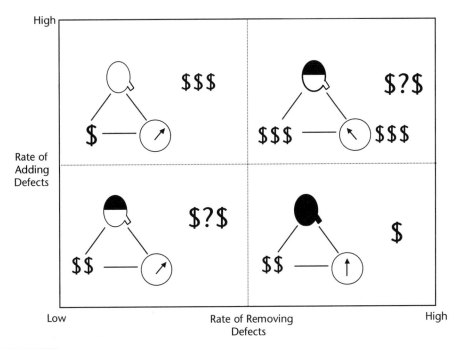

FIGURE 3-1   Defect Add/Remove Rate

project; the cost of rework alone far too often accounts for more than half the cost of production or a project.

Six sigma (like nearly all statistical process improvement/control approaches) looks primarily at the reduction of defect production. At high levels of quality, such as at 6σ, the rate of removal is hardly an issue in the overall cost of quality. The more the production of defects can be reduced, the less significant the cost in time, money, and customer satisfaction created by defects that were not detected and fixed or that were fixed but the fix introduced additional defects that were passed on. Six sigma goes further to eliminate the introduction of defects and reach the implied zero cost for detection and prevention.

SIX SIGMA LEVEL OF QUALITY

A six sigma level of quality is very near perfection. To apply six sigma performance to the goals of better-faster-cheaper would be to say "perfect, instantly, and free." An upside is that if we look at most processes, a significant amount of the time and money spent is for rework or excess production to compensate for rejects and waste. As a generalization, if we change a process to improve the quality of its output, the cost of that process and the time it takes to produce a given amount of acceptable output will also decrease, often significantly. So, while we cannot have things happen instantly or for free, we can demand and achieve perfection or near perfection according to the standards we set to evaluate quality.

Many processes already function at well above six sigma levels of quality. Consider airline safety, for example. Even if commercial flights operated at six sigma, there would be an unacceptable safety risk if we were to define the safety quality metric as defects (crashes involving any fatality) per opportunity (takeoff). If we use the numeric definition of six sigma as 3.4 defects per million opportunities (see Chapter 1), and we look at airline statistics (available at www.airsafetyonline.com/safetycenter/reportcard.shtml), we see that anything even near that defect rate is given a very low score. We also note that airlines at or near that level are those with comparatively few flights; airlines with "A" ratings would have defect rates of a few parts per *billion*.

If we apply this same analysis to other everyday things like the telephone system or the power grid, we find that anything less than at or near perfect performance is unacceptable. Expressed in terms of sigma performance, these activities perform at well above six sigma no matter how we define the numeric values for six sigma.

On the other hand, there are several areas where we, albeit reluctantly, accept performance at very low sigma levels. For example, say we define a defect as a crash of my personal computer and an opportunity as a session where I turn the computer on and expect to do some work (say nominally once per day at 5 days per week). If my PC performed at the level of six sigma evaluated as 3.4 parts per million, then at six sigma performance, I would experience a crash once every 1,170 or so years. Even at 3 sigma, I would experience less than one crash per year. The reality is that I am happy to have a *day* without any crashes.

That brings up another interesting point. If I had the latest in operating systems, without argument I would have fewer crashes. On the other hand, I have to use a tool for one part of my work that apparently will not work right with the latest operating system. (I am forcing the point a little, since there are some more recent workarounds.) So would I have better performance with the new system under my old definition of opportunities and defects, when in reality the system no longer meets its intended purpose—that is, I cannot use it as I need to for at least that one task? Thus, although we are addressing six sigma as a goal, it cannot be the only goal.

Six sigma as a goal offers an organization a lot of attractive advantages. It does not prescribe anything, except results. It does not force non-native disciplines on any aspect of the operations of an organization; it does not, for example, require finance to adopt concepts, disciplines, or methods used in manufacturing. It does not preclude doing anything that might otherwise result in improvement of processes; all it does is gauge the results of improvement efforts and the performance of processes.

There are also disadvantages to just setting a goal and leaving those with responsibility for achieving it without much guidance. Some elements of the organization may need more specific instruction to move effectively toward improved quality. Numerous commercial offerings are available to help with six sigma, some of which may be very expensive in their upfront costs, with no guarantee of an adequate return on investment to the organization. Very often, where total organizational focus is needed for success, leaving the various parts of the organization to implement their disparate methods invites or even ensures at least partial failure.

Any variant of six sigma that an organization may decide to adopt involves some training for everyone in the organization, and considerable training for several people identified as key in the implementation and practice of six sigma. In what is currently the most common variation of six sigma, a martial arts approach is used where individuals earn "belts" of different colors to signify their level of expertise and accomplishment (see Chapter 4). For example, the manager of a six sigma improvement project would be required to have earned a six sigma black belt before being appointed the manager of that project.

Without strong guidance and control of the definitions and collection of the measurements, invalid results may be reported. As an example, I once reviewed a group that was probably working at significantly less than 3 sigma before any type of measurement was instituted. After developing erroneous definitions of defects and opportunities, they could have "pulled the plug" on the service they provided and gone home, and still reported higher than a 5 sigma performance level. While this is probably an extreme case, it does show the need for at least some management control of efforts to achieve a six sigma quality goal.

The key to success with most organizational initiatives is not so much what you undertake to do, but that you are willing to—and actually do— readily abandon what you have done in the past.

CHAPTER 4

Six Sigma "by the Belts"

Current discussions surrounding six sigma often include references to martial arts terminology, such as "black belt" or "green belt," in describing some of the roles assigned to participants. How these roles are incorporated will vary from organization to organization, but it is very likely that the success of six sigma depends on the extent to which the implementing organization structures itself around the disciplines promoted by the six sigma philosophy.

Six sigma projects are those chartered to improve the quality of existing processes. So in an organization that is somewhat project-oriented, there may be a mix of "regular" and six sigma projects. Black belts manage the six sigma projects. Becoming a six sigma black belt is not unlike becoming a black belt in any of the martial arts. It takes training, discipline, and practice. There are several certification programs, not unlike the project management professional (PMP®) or similar project management certifications, for the six sigma black belt.

Although the amount and content of six sigma black belt training varies widely, it will include extensive exposure to and practice with the statistical tools associated with six sigma. Some project managers may choose not to become six sigma black belts, while some six sigma black belts may choose not to become general project managers or, for that matter, to pursue any project management certifications.

The role of the "green belt" is somewhat similar to that of the black belt, but it is generally not a full-time position. For a six sigma project, most of the project team will likely be trained as green belts. Green belt training is often provided to executives and managers who will not be participating directly in six sigma projects, but who need a good understanding of the processes and implications of six sigma.

The "master" black belt is also a full-time position, but primary responsibility lies in providing training and guidance to the organization in general and to the other six sigma participants. Master black belts also are generally better versed in the advanced tools associated with statistical process control and the analysis and interpretation of data.

Black belts are the people in the organization with the training and experience to lead the projects that will change processes. In reality, most organizations already have people in place with roles and experience similar to the black or green belts incorporated in the six sigma process. They may be in the quality organizations, industrial engineering, or project management offices, and are likely already performing many of the functions outlined in the guidance materials for six sigma. All that is needed is for the leadership to commit the organization to achieving six sigma levels of performance and to providing the associated education and training.

CHAPTER 5

Implementing a Formal Six Sigma Program

Several authors, consulting and professional organizations, and practitioners have developed a version of six sigma that recognizes six sigma as a metric, sets six sigma quality as a goal, and goes on to prescribe the organizational structure, tools, and methods needed to implement and achieve higher levels of quality. Implementing six sigma in this context involves a considerable amount of training and coaching as well as many organic changes to the organization and how it operates. Even the "traditional" project manager does not have a defined role without some significant indoctrination into the six sigma program.

The metric in six sigma is standardized: what is called a "mean shift" is specified at 1.5 standard deviations, used in calculating the defect density levels associated with the level of sigma. This largely reflects the manufacturing origins of six sigma, but it also has the effect of making the measurement and math easier as well as incorporating some of the practical realities of achieving very high levels of quality.

For example, if we were to look at a turning operation and measure the diameter of the pieces produced, it is likely that the initial piece produced by the new tool will be at the very bottom of the spec limit, that is, at or near the minimum allowable diameter. As more pieces are produced, the tool will wear and the same machine settings will produce turning of larger and larger diameter, until it is time to readjust the machine or replace the tool. For any given amount of tool wear, the output diameter of the parts produced will have a different mean than for any other state of tool wear. Over the course of a "run," the mean diameter of the parts produced will shift, as in our example of the turning operation, with the mean diameter increasing as the run progresses.

Allowing for the mean shift of $\pm 1.5\sigma$, Figure 5-1 shows the defects as defects per million opportunities (DPMO) for various levels of sigma.

Success in implementing and achieving six sigma depends on the commitment of the organization. We have seen that sigma quality is an executive-

Sigma Level	Defects/Million Opportunities (DPMO)
0	> 941,000
1	693,000
2	308,000
3	67,000
4	6,200
5	230
6	3

FIGURE 5-1   Relationship between Sigma Levels and Defect Densities

type metric. We have discussed six sigma as a goal. We have seen that the sigma level of performance is a property of that process that can be measured. But how can we influence and improve the process to achieve six sigma or better levels of quality?

Six sigma as commonly practiced incorporates six themes to guide an organization's activity to achieve six sigma levels of quality:

- Focus on the customer
- Data- and fact-driven management
- Process focus on management and improvement
- Proactive management
- Boundaryless collaboration
- Drive for perfection, tolerance for failure.

FOCUS ON THE CUSTOMER

Focus on the customer is one of the key elements of six sigma, and it is critical.

It is not likely that the customer really cares to know the overall sigma level of your processes and products. Customers do not really care how many defects or defects per million opportunities are in your products or services. Customers care that the products work for what they intend to use them for or that the services meet their needs or provide the benefits they seek when they request the service.

Customers generally are not impressed with high levels of customer support quality in support of unreliable products. If the focus is kept on the customer, quality levels and sigma levels will certainly improve. It is not uncommon that where the focus is on a metric or on measures of performance, the customer becomes subordinated to responses that threaten or do not affect the in-place measures of performance. It is commonly said that "activity flows toward measurement." In six sigma, the activity must flow toward the satisfaction of the customer.

Having customers is not the natural result of having high levels of quality performance. In fact, it works the other way around: having high levels of quality is the natural result of having customers and focusing on their needs.

DATA- AND FACT-DRIVEN MANAGEMENT

Despite the common admonishment to manage by "facts and data," most organizations do a very poor job of identifying the data they need to support decisions that will significantly advance their organization's effectiveness. Most data collected are "passive data"—the result of something inherent in the process or the tools used. Very little effort is required to collect these data and they are often incorporated into numerous reports and analyses. This "bottom up" approach to data—trying to make useful information from data that are readily available and easy to collect—more often results in making the wrong decisions or in missing opportunities for making improvements or avoiding problems.

Six sigma incorporates a top-down approach to identifying information requirements. Much like in a stakeholder analysis,[1] first the customers of the measurement are identified and solicited for their information needs. Then that information is used to develop the measurement plan.

Since the sigma metrics are really only a measure of results, the vast majority of the measurement activity is focused on information that will help the organization understand and improve the processes that must be changed to achieve higher levels of quality. Six sigma is an executive-level metric. In a metrics program that has three levels of metrics—operating or tactical metrics at the lowest level, managerial metrics at the middle level, and executive or strategic metrics at the top level—many more metrics at each lower level are needed to support the decisions that will influence the behavior of the related metrics at the higher levels of the measurement hierarchy.

PROCESS FOCUS ON MANAGEMENT AND IMPROVEMENT

It usually brings smiles when we define insanity as "doing the same thing and expecting different results," but it ceases to be so funny when one watches over and over as organizations demand improvement but do not commit to understanding and changing processes.

Process presents one of the greatest challenges for project managers to identify with six sigma. Are projects processes? We tend to think of processes as sets of steps in an order that are repeated, and indeed that is the most common and most practical definition. Also, the definition of a project alludes to its one-time nature, so with the most rigorous use of the definitions of the terms, instead of a *process* we use a *plan*, which is then executed with modification as indicated and needed.

In general, once any part of the plan is complete, it is probably not used, or at least not on that project. If it is used in subsequent projects, it very likely will be modified. It is in the nature of projects that subsequent projects, however similar, are likely to be executed in a different context (i.e., place, people, and tools) to the point where the assumption that this iteration is the same as preceding ones would introduce risk.

Since we consider the sigma quality level to be a property of any product or process, we could actually try to measure and improve it for everything. In measurement, I have defined the "Mount Everest Theory of Measurement" where everything is measured "because it's there." Programs that incorporate this theory generally fail because they cost considerably more than the benefits they deliver. Arguably, it is possible to achieve six sigma in any activity. However, there is a cost associated with measuring and improving processes and a benefit associated with the improvements that can also be quantified. Quite often the cost of achieving six sigma quality for some processes exceeds the benefits that performance at that level will provide.

Perfection in project management does not necessarily mean that all projects were completed on time and budget and met or exceeded their quality objectives. Six sigma is largely "deterministic." That is, one can, with reasonable accuracy and reliability, identify the sigma level for a process and rely on the expectation that until the process changes, the results of the process performance will stay the same.

On the other hand, projects are largely "probabilistic." Whether a project is a true success or failure depends on several factors that are evaluated as risks that may or may not occur. Even the definition of success varies in projects. For some projects, success may mean the timely termination of the project with no results delivered other than the knowledge that the purpose of the project was unattainable or that the initial assumptions were wrong.

Six sigma focuses on the "good" or the quality aspect of "good-fast-cheap" and assumes that we have a commitment to improve all three for our processes. Projects often have an absolute constraint in one or two of the dimensions and it is not often possible to invest the time or money and still meet the constraints on the project.

The first opportunity is to think of project management as a process itself. Although modified, adapted, and scaled to some extent for each project, a significant amount of the project management "process" is common to any project. There are also enough aspects to each of these common steps that it is possible that defects and opportunities for defects can be defined meaningfully and usefully.

Defects do not have to be hard measures like the diameter plus or minus the tolerance. They can be soft measures, like an opinion from a survey or an acceptance consensus from a checklist. What is important is to maintain the focus on the customer and, if you can, establish measurable aspects of your project management processes that ultimately result in improvements that the customer recognizes.

The second opportunity is to think of the processes incorporated in any project in terms of the capabilities used in the project. Normally we think of a process as a fixed capability with a variable throughput and defined capacities. For projects (or any "customized process,") we should think of the process as variable capabilities with defined throughputs and "adequate" capacity. By establishing utilization factors, such as if and how much a particular capability is used for any project, an analyst can effectively define, measure, analyze, improve, and control any "ad hoc" process.

PROACTIVE MANAGEMENT

None of these themes is really new with six sigma, but together they are the key factors of success for any approach to improvement, be it by the leaders such as Motorola or by the followers that have realized considerable improvements by following the lead of others. There will always be a few organizations that "hit the lottery" and have to react to their unexpected success, but most must create their own success. Even then, closer examination will reveal that those that seemed to have a broad stroke of luck could only react for a short while and had to become proactive to continue their success.

The very best that can be expected with reactive management is to maintain the status quo. Usually what must be accepted is the mitigation of loss and damage.

The six sigma measure is a gauge of improvement. If—and this is a big element of the reality of implementing six sigma—the sigma-level results can be determined objectively, they are a valid indicator of change. With proactive management, the sigma-quality level will change (statistically) significantly with time. The level may even go down, since risk is always associated with proactive management behavior, but in the long run, six sigma identifies proactive management. Six sigma inherently sets the goals for the level of proactive management, and the organization must set its own goals for the rate at which those goals are achieved.

BOUNDARYLESS COLLABORATION

"Boundaryless collaboration" is one area where traditional project managers will excel. Traditional organizations have typically spent years building boundaries between their various locations and subunits. It is not unusual to find as much or more competition between the various divisions as there is between the organization and its competitors.

Even in organizations where projects are few, the project managers always must figure out how to work across these boundaries to make everything the project includes happen on time and within budget. In organizations where projects are more common, it is not unusual to find formalized variation of "matrix management," where formal relationships and processes are set up between the vertical divisions of the organization and the cross-functional needs of projects.

Six sigma is an "organic change" for any organization that adopts it. That is, it will require changes that are universal and significant. One change program adopted the slogan "every day in every way" to describe the extent of the change envisioned. Six sigma involves such change. Those who are unwilling or unable to change will be left behind or forced elsewhere—where they no longer detract from the change mandated by achieving the goals.

Six sigma also means that roles must change. Where there were many levels of management, there might be fewer. Certain skills may no longer be useful while other skills that were not part of the old organization will be required.

One powerful aspect of the level of formalization for six sigma is that there are considerable opportunities for training as well as for certifications for some of the roles defined for the six sigma organization. Six sigma is not usually presented like a prescription or cookbook for success. The approach is based more on creating the right organization for improvement and achieving six sigma quality, primarily by creating an organization of highly trained professionals who understand how to achieve six sigma levels of quality and are led and facilitated in doing so.

Boundaryless collaboration is not limited to within the organization implementing six sigma. For many years we have been concerned with supply chain management (SCM), or in working more closely with the organization's suppliers to ensure better efficiency and quality. Much has also been written and done about customer relationship management (CRM), which is aimed at improving communications with customers to focus on their needs and on their satisfaction with the goods and services they are provided.

Research on these topics most often focuses on the technology of the communications, databases, and tools that will provide better SCM and CRM. In actuality, managing suppliers and customers is much more than just a technical problem requiring alignment of goals, strategies, and an organization in a concerted focus on the needs of the customer with an objective and comprehensive assessment of how well those needs are being met. Six sigma provides the foundation for SCM and CRM to work effectively because it brings the organization and its suppliers into focus with customer needs, unobstructed by the artificial boundaries that tend to establish themselves in the absence of a six sigma type of discipline.

DRIVE FOR PERFECTION, TOLERANCE FOR FAILURE

Even if you find the math that underlies six sigma unclear, it should be clear that six sigma, for all intents and purposes, represents perfection. Or at least from the perspective of defects, six sigma is essentially zero defects.

What is also clear is that in six sigma, defects are not tolerated. There is no "good enough," no "running out of improvement budget," no slowing or stopping improvement if an interim goal is neared or reached; there is only continuous improvement. In six sigma there is no "sandbagging" improvement to "look good" in later reporting periods; there is only focus on the ultimate customer of the improved products or services.

Any process has what is called its "capacity." We usually think of capacity as "how much," but capacity also applies to "how well." If we reach the capacity for how much a process will produce and still need it to produce more, we must either add more channels (i.e., replicate the process) or change the process so it has a higher output capacity. Likewise, when a process is at its capacity to produce output free of defects and we need fewer defects, we must change the process (as replication would only produce more at the same rate of defects).

For example, we may observe that a process can only produce 1,000 units per hour. We may also observe that it has a performance level of 3 sigma. We may observe that we can get a maximum output of 1,200 units per hour but the quality level drops to 2.8 sigma. We may also notice that we can reduce the output to 900 units per hour and increase the quality to 3.5 sigma. But there is a relationship inherent in the process that defines the limits of throughput and quality such that there is both a relationship and an upper limit to both the output and the quality of the output. Higher levels of either cannot be achieved without significantly changing the process or implementing a substantially new process.

Normally, continuous improvement implies many small changes to move a process toward its quality capacity. "Innovation" is the term usually used for making significant changes that result in change to the quality capacity of a process. With these definitions, continuous improvement is operating in "charted territory" while innovation is "boldly going where no one has gone before."

Of course, innovation requires some degree of risk, which would include failure. Even where an innovation has the potential to improve performance significantly, it is not at all uncommon for the initial results to be worse than what the innovation is intended to replace.

Just as the functional division was an observed common characteristic for traditional organizations, a fear of failure is common in traditional organizations. The "tyranny" of the performance review has gone a long way toward making many managers and leaders risk-averse by generally rewarding maintaining the status quo or by successfully mitigating loss and damage (reactive management), while punishing or at least failing to reward innovation that failed in some respect or even that was not immediately evident in its success.

The six sigma process is defined to ensure continuous improvement. Six sigma incorporates *define, measure, analyze, improve,* and *control* (DMAIC) as the continuing cycle that yields improvement and ultimately achieves six sigma levels of quality performance:

- *Define.* In this step, the opportunity for quality improvement is identified and described. The customers are identified, both for the project and for the business processes involved. The project boundaries and scope are defined as well. A detailed description and a mapping of the process to be improved are also prepared.

- *Measure.* A data collection plan is prepared for the existing process and data are collected to determine the performance of the process. Customers of the process should also be solicited for their input related to the performance of the process.

- *Analyze.* Using the data and the process definitions and maps created in the design step, process changes are identified that will reduce or eliminate the defects produced by the process. Any measures and metrics that will validate or help control the improved process are also identified and incorporated into the measurement plan.

- *Improve.* This is the actual implementation of the changes to the process being improved. This area presents an opportunity for the use of traditional project managers, or at least of black belts with traditional project management education and experience, and perhaps even certification. The approach will reduce the risk of project failure, especially where the project is particularly large or involves significant change to existing processes.

- *Control.* There is a dual meaning for control in six sigma, or in any form of statistical process control. The first meaning of control is when to do something (and, of course, what and where and how much). If there is an indication that something is out of control, then it is incumbent on those responsible for the process to take action that will restore the performance to an in-control condition. The second, and often more important, meaning of control is knowing when to do nothing. Expect variation, but more importantly, know how much variation to expect. When observed variation exceeds the expected variation and the indicators can be confirmed to be accurate, there is a near certainty of a special cause of variation and the need for a special action to identify and correct or compensate for the special cause.

SUCCESSFUL SIX SIGMA IMPLEMENTATION

While this formal six sigma approach is but one of several versions of six sigma improvement, the six themes that underlie a successful six sigma implementation are what is really important:

Focus on the customer. Customers will ultimately define the success of the improvements, as demonstrated by their loyalty or their departure. Failure or success for six sigma ultimately turns on the ability to impress and thus capture and retain loyal customers. It is clear that we can focus six sigma on the absence of defects in products and services, but if we limit the definitions of defects to those things inherent in the products or services we deliver, we are at risk of limiting the potential of our focus on the customer to the limitations of our products and services. So, what we can deliver to our customer or potential customer may be free of defects by any way in which we can view it, but from the customer's or potential customer's perspective, if it does not meet their needs, the absence of defects is of no consequence.

It is important to define categories of defects that have a basis in customer needs and not just those inherent in our products and services. So say, for example, I produce automobiles and it is clear from my marketing assessment information that the most desired cruising range (average distance on a tank of gas) is 350 miles. I can produce an automobile at a six sigma level of quality for all of the technical specifications, but it only has a cruising range of 250 miles. It is clear that I have focused on the product and have met my quality goals, but I have not met the customer's quality goals, because I am deficient on the one key point of the cruising range.

Data- and fact-driven management. Six sigma is a quantitative method supported by the judicious use of data and facts derived from data. One of the greatest challenges to the success of six sigma is the insistence by leaders that decisions once made without the support of quantitative evidence are now either made only with great reluctance or deferred until they can be supported. Many programs fail not because they fail to embrace the future, but because they fail to abandon the past. If decisions that can be made in the light of facts and data are also still made in the absence of facts and data, such as "on the golf course" or on the basis of "favors owed" or "politics," or if it is apparent that the facts and data have no real influence on the outcome of decisions, the initiative will quickly fail.

Process focus on management and improvement. Six sigma is built on the foundations of statistical process control and provides tools that work to improve the performance of current and future iterations of a process. Although it is not common for projects or for highly project-oriented organizations to have a high dependence on processes, the advanced methods of recognizing the process nature of project work are necessary to ensure that the benefits of six sigma are recognized in all areas where they will benefit the organization the most. It is true that some projects are nearly 100% unique—that what is done in and by the project has not been done before and, if the project is a success, it will not likely be done again. But, it is much more likely that the differences between any current project and past or future projects are not so great and there is a considerable opportunity for improvements in performance and quality by recognizing and managing the similarities using tools like those associated with six sigma, just as the project management tools are used to manage the unique points of the projects.

Proactive management. Six sigma methods and tools clearly distinguish the improvement realized in performance over time. The imperative to improve and the goals for improvement established by the leaders of the organization will clearly identify where proactive management is the practice. So what is proactive management? Is it the opposite of reactive management, which we might think of as something negative or not as good as proactive management? Is it something more akin to "empowerment," where management has unprecedented levels of autonomy? In reality it is more of the nature of some of the problems where we are at a loss for a precise definition but we "know it when we see it."

Deming's point about driving out fear is akin to the practice of proactive management. Managers must not fear making a decision that will affect the performance of anything within the scope of their responsibility. There must be no fear of making a mistake. The six sigma methods provide a clear indication of where a mistake has been made, so its correction can be identified as easily as it was to make the mistake in the first place. What has to be clear is that no improvements can happen without changes. Big improvements almost always require big changes.

Boundaryless collaboration. Six sigma is not unique in recognizing the problems associated with organizational boundaries and internal competition. Project managers are most likely among the better versed in seeing the need for a cross-functional team or integration that avoids the politics that can accompany the challenge to accomplish a project's goals. Boundaries can also exist between the suppliers and customers associated with a project, and six sigma encourages and provides the tools for working effectively across those boundaries as well.

To borrow from the metaphor that a rising tide raises all boats, six sigma is not about competition between the boats, but about all the boats cooperating to raise the tide (if that is possible) or to ensure that the implied benefit from the rising tide is realized as best as possible by all boats as a whole and by the individual boats as best suited for each.

Drive for perfection, tolerance for failure. For all intents and purposes, six sigma is perfect performance. With few exceptions, achieving six sigma requires significant changes not just in processes, but in the organization's culture, in the people within the organization, in the physical plant where the processes are performed, and possibly in many other areas, any of which may introduce considerable risk for the project chartered to implement the change. Even where projects succeed, changed processes usually have learning curve dynamics associated with them: the measure of performance is worse at the outset but improves as the process is "learned" or absorbed by the system in which it operates. Fear of failure must be driven out if the courage to take the risks that will yield significant improvement is expected.

The six sigma process of define, measure, analyze, improve, and control (DMAIC) guides six sigma improvement activity. In the *define* step, the process to be improved is identified and documented, and the scope of the project and the stakeholders are defined. The *measure* step establishes the benchmark against which the improvements will be validated. The *analyze* step identifies the changes that will be made in the process being improved. In general project management terms, this step creates the plan. Also in general project management terms, *improve* is the execution phase where the planned changes are actually implemented. *Control* is the follow-on phase where the changed process is stabilized and the improvements are validated against the benchmarks identified for the old process.

Many organizations have significantly improved their positions in their markets or in their roles using the principles and tools of a formal six sigma program. The key to success is in the leadership that commits the organization to do something radically different while ceasing to do things in the old ways. Six sigma is the philosophy and the tool set that should help any organization to do just that.

NOTE

1. Steve Neuendorf, *Project Measurement* (Vienna, VA: Management Concepts, Inc., 2002). © 2002, Management Concepts, Inc.

CHAPTER 6

"Ultimate" Six Sigma

Although there are as many versions of six sigma as there are practitioners, one major variant from the common state of the practice is called "ultimate six sigma," largely as promoted by Keki Bhote in his book *The Ultimate Six Sigma: Beyond Quality Excellence to Total Business Excellence*.[1] Bhote was instrumental in Motorola's original conception and implementation of six sigma in the early 1980s. His observations of numerous companies unsuccessfully trying to implement six sigma at the hands of opportunistic consulting companies compelled him to publish what amounts to the latest major work regarding the implementation of six sigma. His book offers considerable insight into significantly improving quality and overall performance.

As described by Bhote, the objectives of ultimate six sigma are to:

- Develop a comprehensive infrastructure that goes well beyond the narrow confines of quality to encompass all areas of business excellence.
- Maximize all stakeholder loyalty: customer loyalty, employee loyalty, supplier loyalty, distributor/dealer loyalty, and investor loyalty.
- Maximize business results: profits, return on investment, asset turns, inventory turns, sales/value-added per employee.
- Minimize turnover and bring joy to the workplace, especially to the line worker.
- Go beyond modest and mediocre quality standards/systems to devise an ideal yet practical quality system.
- Go beyond the tired problem-solving tools of the twentieth century to forge powerful new tools for the twenty-first century.
- Go beyond the propaganda and results-with-mirrors of the hyped six sigma consulting companies to usher in ultimate six sigma, which is low in implementation costs and high in business results.

- Provide keys to critical success factors in each of twelve areas:
  1. Customer loyalty and long-term retention
  2. Quality of leadership (to provide vision and inspiration, which facilitate employees reaching their full potential)
  3. Quality of organization (to revolutionize the ways people are hired, trained, evaluated, compensated, and promoted)
  4. Quality of employees (to provide empowerment on the road to industrial democracy)
  5. Quality of metrics (to assess business excellence)
  6. Quality of tools (to achieve quality, cost, and cycle-time breakthroughs)
  7. Quality of design (to maximize customer value and the "wow" factor)
  8. Quality of supplier partnerships (to improve customer quality, cost, and cycle time while enhancing supplier profits)
  9. Quality of manufacturing (i.e., overall) effectiveness
  10. Quality of field reliability (toward zero field failures)
  11. Quality of support service (i.e., business/white-collar) effectiveness
  12. Quality of results (to develop and rate world-class metrics).
- Conduct periodic audits and self-assessments to achieve continuous, never-ending improvement.

BENEFITS OF ULTIMATE SIX SIGMA

Concentrating on the principles, methodologies, and actions Bhote describes in *The Ultimate Six Sigma* will enable a company to create metrics for business, customer loyalty, and quality. According to Bhote, the benefits of each of these metrics are as follows.

Business Metrics

- Enhance the business's long-term profits by factors of 2:1 to 5:1 and from 4 percent to 20 percent of sales (after tax).
- Enhance return on investment by 3:1 to 8:1 and from 10–15 percent to more than 50 percent.
- Enhance asset turns from 4 to over 15.
- Increase inventory turns from 6–10 to more than 100.
- Reduce people turnover from 20 percent to 10 percent, and eventually down to less than 0.5 percent per year.

- Increase productivity (i.e., value-added) per employee per year from $100,000 by 30 percent, eventually to more than $500,000.

Customer Loyalty Metrics

- Improve customer loyalty and retention levels from below 75 percent to 99 percent.
- Increase customer retention longevity from less than 5 years to over 15 years.
- Increase the satisfaction rating of all stakeholders by 2:1 to over 90 percent.
- Increase market share position to number one or two in each business line.

Quality/Reliability/Cycle Time Metrics

- Reduce outgoing defect rates from the 1–10 percent range down to 10 parts per million (ppm) and lower.
- Reduce total defects per unit (TDPU) on an entire product line from the 1–5 range down to 0.1.
- Increase c_{p_k} [a measure of process capability to meet customer requirements] of critical parameters from the 0.5–1.0 range up to 2.0–5.0.
- Reduce field failures from the 2–20 percent range per year down to 100 ppm per year.
- Reduce the cost of poor quality (as a percent of sales dollars) from the 8–20 percent range down to less than one percent.
- Reduce cycle times in production and business processes (in multiplies of theoretical cycle time—that is, direct labor time) from the 10–100 range down to 1.5–2.0.[2]

The benefits Bhote attributes to ultimate six sigma are not theoretical, but rather are based on actual experience for organizations making a complete and total commitment to improvement using the six sigma methods. Like six sigma "by the belts," ultimate six sigma can be evaluated by looking at the organization that supports its implementation and the processes and tools incorporated.

In addition, ultimate six sigma relies on a set of tools to effect its implementation and to realize the expected results and benefits. Of greatest importance to the project manager working in an organization that is either implementing or operating under a program based on ultimate six sigma is the ability to understand the nature and use of these tools and their application at the project level. Bhote introduces the ultimate six sigma self-assessment chart and scoring system (see Figures 6-1, 6-2, and 6-3).

Area	Key Characteristics	Importance (Points)
1. Customer		<u>125</u>
	1.1 Importance of Customer Loyalty	20
	1.2 Inviolate Principles of Customer Loyalty	25
	1.3 Customer Differentiation	30
	1.4 Customer Requirement	15
	1.5 Company Structure for Customer Loyalty	20
	1.6 Defection Management Control	5
	1.7 Public as Customer	10
2. Leadership		<u>125</u>
	2.1 Personal Philosophies and Values	60
	2.2 Corporate Principles	30
	2.3 The Corporate Role of Leadership	35
3. Organization		<u>75</u>
	3.1 Dismantling Taylorism	10
	3.2 Revolutionizing the Organizational Culture	65
4. Employees		<u>75</u>
	4.1 Motivation: From "How to" to "Want to"	20
	4.2 Job Security	5
	4.3 Empowerment Readiness	5
	4.4 Team Competition	5
	4.5 Empowerment Systems	35
	4.6 Empowerment Stage	5
5. Measurement		<u>75</u>
	5.1 Measurement Axioms	5
	5.2 Measurement Principles	30
	5.3 Financial Statements	5
	5.4 Core Customers	10
	5.5 Generic Measurements	20
	5.6 Team/Department Measurements	5
6. Tools for the 21st Century		<u>75</u>
	6.1 Design of Experiments	15
	6.2 Multiple Environment Over Stress Test	10
	6.3 Mass Customization/Quality Function Deployment	10
	6.4 Total Productive Maintenance	5
	6.5 Benchmarking	5
	6.6 Poka-Yoke	5
	6.7 Business Process Reengineering and Next Operation as Customer	10
	6.8 Total Value Engineering	5
	6.9 Supply Chain Management	5
	6.10 Lean Manufacturing/Inventory/Cycle Time Reduction	5

FIGURE 6-1   Ultimate Six Sigma Self-Assessment Chart

Area	Key Characteristics	Importance (Points)
7. Design	7.1 Organization for New Product Introduction 7.2 Management Guidelines 7.3 Voice of the Customer 7.4 Design Quality/Reliability 7.5 Design for Cost Reduction 7.6 Design for Cycle Time Reduction	<u>75</u> 5 5 10 25 15 15
8. Supply Chain Management	8.1 Importance of Supply Chain Management 8.2 Supply Partnership Principles 8.3 Types of Mutual Help 8.4 Selection of Partnership Suppliers 8.5 Infrastructure 8.6 Supplier Development	<u>75</u> 15 10 5 15 15 15
9. Manufacturing	9.1 Manufacturing Resurgence 9.2 Quality Improvement in Manufacturing 9.3 Cycle Time Reduction in Manufacturing	<u>75</u> 10 40 25
10. Field Operations	10.1 Product Reliability 10.2 Predelivery Services 10.3 Services to Downstream Supply Chain 10.4 Services to User	<u>75</u> 15 15 20 25
11. Service Industries/ Support Services in Manufacturing	11.1 Basic Principles of Next Operations as [Customer] (NOAC) 11.2 NOAC Structure 11.3 NOAC Implementation	<u>75</u> 30 30 15
12. Results	12.1 Customers 12.2 Leadership 12.3 Employees 12.4 Financials	<u>75</u> 20 20 20 15

FIGURE 6-1   Ultimate Six Sigma Self-Assessment Chart (cont'd.)

Rating	Criteria
1	No knowledge of the success factor
2	Only a conceptual awareness of the success factor
3	Success factor started, with less than 50% implementation
4	Success factor 50% to 80% implemented
5	Success factor implementation more than 80% complete, along with reflected business results

FIGURE 6-2   Success Factor Rating

Total Company Rating	Equivalent Business Health	Equivalent Sigma Level
800–1,000	Robust health	6 Sigma
600–799	Good health, but periodic physical checkups (audits) urged	5 Sigma
400–599	Poor health; continual monitoring needed	4 Sigma
200–399	Major surgery needed	3 Sigma
Below 200	Terminally ill	2 Sigma

FIGURE 6-3   Total Rating: A Corresponding Business Health and Equivalent Sigma Level

The ultimate six sigma self-assessment chart and scoring system provide an indication of the comprehensive nature of six sigma and of the relative importance of many of the items considered. In his book Bhote provides sub-forms for each of the areas. The intent of the assessment is that it will be completed by trained and objective outside assessors.

It is important to note that the customer and leadership categories significantly outweigh the other categories. Also, as indicated in Figure 6-3, a sigma level can be associated with the general sigma score that would be expected to be observed from direct measurement.

Another important area for project managers interested in ultimate six sigma is what are called the 21st century tools in question area 6 of the assessment (see Figure 6-1). With a little experience or a minimum of research, you would quickly recognize that none of these tools is new nor are the tools particularly associated with six sigma, although Bhote has proposed significant improvements to the design of experiments (DOE) tool.

Although these tools are neither new nor unique to any version of six sigma, the conceptualization of six sigma brings them together in a focused program. Very much like the collection of "best practices" commonly sought in management initiatives, it is the context in which they are applied that determines how good they really are. The same applies to six sigma: the notion of implementing six sigma in a cookbook fashion or that one size fits all is a likely recipe for failure.

The tools from question 6 in the assessment are each powerful and would be worthwhile for further investigation by any project manager who recognizes their potential application.

The first tool is the DOE method. While there are several variants of the DOE tool, the one outlined here is the Shainin/Bhote variation. Twelve techniques are associated with this variation of the DOE tool, many of which originated in the general field of quality assurance:

1. *Multi-Vari:* Reduce the large number of unmanageable variables to a smaller group of related variables.
2. *Components Search:* Swap parts and subassemblies between best and worst products to quickly and neatly identify the root causes of failure.
3. *Paired Comparisons:* Compare a group of eight of the best products (the number relates to statistical significance) with a group of the eight worst products to distinguish the important quality characteristics from the less important ones.
4. *Product/Process Search:* Separate the important process parameters that produce good and bad products from the unimportant ones.
5. *Variables Search:* Pinpoint the important variables. Consider opening up the tolerances on the unimportant variables to reduce costs.
6. *Full Factorial:* An experimental alternative to the variables search where there are four or fewer variables to be considered. The variables are "forced" to all possible combinations of high and low in an experimental production run and the results are analyzed.
7. *B versus C:* Verify that a better (B) product or process where an improvement has been made over a current (C) product or process constitutes a permanent improvement with at least a 95% confidence.
8. *Scatter Plot:* Determine realistic specifications and realistic tolerances for important variables. (Author's note: It is not that uncommon that six sigma "levels of quality" are reached by measuring bogus variables with inconsequential tolerance levels.)
9. *Response Surface Methodology (RSM):* This has the same objective as a scatter plot, but is a more appropriate tool where there is significant interaction between two or more variables.
10. *Positrol:* A tool and method set for controlling variables during production.
11. *Process Certification:* Another tool and method set used to increase the signal-to-noise ratio in experiments.
12. *Precontrol:* A tool similar to control charts, but more effective at ensuring that the quality achieved in the DOE process is maintained in production.

Like the DMAIC of six sigma, a generic problem-solving process is associated with ultimate six sigma, incorporating the DOE tools and methods:[3]

1. Define the problem.
2. Quantify and measure the problem:

- Measure scatter plot (rather than gauge R & R)
- Use Likert scale to convert attributes into variables.
3. Define the problem history (e.g., problem age, defective rate, cost).
4. Generate clues using:
   - Multi-vari (including concentration charts)
   - Components search
   - Paired comparisons
   - Product/process search.
5. Implement formal design of experiments
   - Variables search
   - Full factorials
   - B versus C.
6. Turn the problem on and off to ensure permanency of improvement using:
   - B versus C.
7. Establish realistic specifications and tolerances (optimize) using:
   - Scatter plots (for no interaction effects)
   - Response surface methodology (if there are strong interaction effects).
8. "Freeze" the process improvements using:
   - Positrol.
9. Certify the process, nailing down all peripheral quality issues.
10. Hold the gains with statistical process control (SPC):
    - Precontrol.

ADDITIONAL TOOLS

Bhote outlines several other 21st century tools to help ensure that six sigma levels of quality can be achieved and maintained.

Multiple Environment over Stress Testing

Multiple environment over stress testing (MOEST) actually considers the customer beyond products being free of defects. To the customer, reliability is usually more important than quality as measured by DPMO. Time and stress will take its toll on an otherwise perfect product. Where reliability is important, the MOEST method should be investigated and employed.

Mass Customization and Quality Function Deployment

The methods of mass customization and quality function deployment (QFD) are both aimed at engaging the customer. For mass customization, it is necessary to figure out how to provide each customer with the product that will provide lifetime value, as opposed to identifying economical production runs or delivery methods that really only satisfy "average" customer needs (as the earlier statistical discussion showed, only a very few are really "average") and focus on meeting each customer's needs precisely.

Where mass customization focuses on production, QFD focuses on the design of the product or service. Like some of the other tools in this group, QFD is a somewhat structured and detailed method of ensuring that the features identified as "quality" by the customer (as opposed to those identified by engineers or marketing people) are actually incorporated into the design of the product or service. When you hear the term "house of quality," it is in reference to a QFD method.

Total Productive Maintenance

It is not enough that a process is able to produce high-quality, defect-free output; the process also must be capable of being executed efficiently as often as needed or, in many cases, continuously with little or no down time. Down time can be a killer to profits and performance for organizations that depend on physical plant. If the reliability of production capability is important, the total productive maintenance (TPM) method warrants investigation.

Benchmarking

Enough cannot be said about the power of benchmarking, yet so few practice it at all and even many who try do not do it effectively. Benchmarking is a way of comparing your processes and results with those of others. Benchmarking can be done internally or externally. Many things you may already be doing, such as belonging to industry associations or professional societies, are forms of benchmarking, and there may only be a few simple steps remaining to realize the full potential of this technique.

Bhote offers the following concise benchmarking road map:[4]

1. Define why and what to benchmark.
2. Establish your own company's baseline.
3. Perform pilot runs in your company and adjacent companies.
4. Identify whom to benchmark.
5. Visit benchmark companies.
6. Determine the performance gap between your company and the benchmark company.
7. Secure top management commitment.
8. Establish goals and action plans.

9. Implement plans and monitor results.
10. Recalibrate/recycle the process.

While this approach is formulated for "external results" benchmarking, it would also work if you were benchmarking internally or if you were comparing processes.

Poka-Yoke

Poka-yoke is the practice of "instrumenting" a process so as to warn its operators in a timely fashion that a mistake has been made or is about to be made. It is really as simple as it sounds. This practice reduces dependence on inspection and testing to find defects in products and make a contribution to achieving higher levels of sigma quality.

Business Process Reengineering and Next Operation As Customer

Business process reengineering (BPR) has had a lot of bad press, which can be attributed largely to the often-mistaken assumption that there really is a process and it is the result of something that approximates engineering. However, for business processes that do not lend themselves well to the use of tools like the DOE, BPR can be very effective at improving those processes. It may be worthwhile to consider using BPR for improvement of the "softer" processes.

"Next operation as customer" (NOAC) also defines itself to an extent. It is easy to assume that "focusing on the customer" means focusing on the end customer—those who pay for the result of our products and services. In fact, if the customer is considered to be whoever receives the output of our process or step in the process, greatly improved quality and efficiency can be realized in any process.

Total Value Engineering

Value engineering, a concept that has been around since the 1940s, refers to products being engineered to deliver high levels of value at low levels of cost. Total value engineering goes beyond that definition to focus more fully on the customer and provide the value and reliability needed to foster customer loyalty while reducing costs. To paraphrase a detraction spawned by a quality program that "quality is king but schedule is God," in total value engineering, cost may be king but customer loyalty is God.

Supply Chain Engineering and Lean Manufacturing

Supply chain engineering is closely related to supply chain management (SCM). This concept contends that anything can be viewed and managed as a process. Instead of being ad hoc, processes can be engineered to ensure optimization of performance and quality.

Lean manufacturing tends to imply its own definition, as opposed to "fat manufacturing," with lots of waste and inefficiencies. Improving processes can significantly reduce waste and rework, with substantial reductions in cycle time and cost.

All these tools exist and are used independently of any of the six sigma variants. The underlying principles have much in common, and it still seems that the keys to success are hard work, knowledge, and commitment.

NOTES

1. Keki Bhote, *The Ultimate Six Sigma: Beyond Quality Excellence to Total Business Excellence* (New York, NY: AMACOM, 2002). © 2002, AMACOM.
2. Ibid., pp. 24–26.
3. Ibid., p. 182.
4. Ibid., p. 196.

CHAPTER 7

Applying Six Sigma to Project Management

So how can six sigma be applied to project management?

At the outset, we have noted that a significant number of initiatives fail for a myriad of reasons, most of which can be summed up by noting that the change required is bigger than the organization is really ready to accept. For the purposes of this discussion, let's assume that the people issues and commitment issues that would otherwise foil such a project have been addressed and resolved. Instead, we will focus on the process and measurement issues that the project to implement six sigma for project management must resolve. We will assume that in the organization we are using as an example, project management is not a well-defined and organizationally supported discipline. Moreover, other activity related to six sigma is in the initial stages.

PROCESS ISSUES

Achieving and maintaining six sigma performance really has more to do with project management than with the disciplines of quality control and quality assurance or with process management, or even with the root discipline that is the subject of the performance measures and improvement activity. Of course, all these aspects are significant and necessary, but project management is what holds them all together and serves as the conduit that will ensure that the benefits flow to the bottom line of the organization.

The threshold question is whether or not project management is a process. One could argue that project management goes beyond the trappings of a process to where the judgment of the individual project manager must supersede any definition imposed by traditional process characterization. Consider project management as a profession. A considerable faction of the project management profession, as well as the application of project management, takes the various project management professional certifications into account. Do we apply six sigma in other professions, particularly in the licensed professions? Apparently there is some effort underway in medicine (for example, see www.hopkinsmedicine.org/crossroads/crossroads_12_12.html) and in several other fields. Many organizations have applied six sigma to their internal legal and engineering operations.

Moreover, recent developments in corporate accountability will undoubtedly inspire increased quality activity, much of which will adopt six sigma principles; this can be expected within the accounting professions as well. If we view project management as a profession, six sigma can clearly be applied to project management.

So how would we implement six sigma in project management? Let's begin by considering how six sigma defines the process for doing this, with the generic steps represented in the acronym DMAIC (define, measure, analyze, improve, and control). We would start with "define" as a statement of the problem or condition that identifies the need and desire to change.

Say, for example, that our organization provides no formal structure for project managers. Individual departments define projects where the work is either unique enough that it is not well accommodated by existing processes or where there is significant involvement by other departments. Projects may also be established where the visibility desired is high enough to warrant use of the procedures and accounting normally employed by projects. The individual department will appoint the project manager either from within its own ranks or acquire a new hire or contract employee.

Say the organization decides to implement an independent organization with a charter to provide and facilitate project management needs and to promote the use of projects in the accomplishment of a larger amount of the organization's work. The organization may also decide to establish a project to support the fledgling six sigma initiative underway in other parts of the organization.

The succinct statement of the problem is that the organization does not have a manageable process for meeting its project management needs. Moreover, the organization needs to significantly improve the capability and capacity of its project management resources as well as to develop a high and consistent quality of the project management services provided. Further, the organization needs to establish a capability for the administration and support of project management.

A review process is also needed to enable the organization to assess whether its resources are most appropriately organized and administered as a project. The project management function would be responsible for ensuring the quality of its own performance.

MEASUREMENT ISSUES

What would we need to measure to contrast the conditions within the organization with the goals or objectives inherent in this definition of a project management structure?

The first part of the definition looks at the organizational need for some project management-related function. Aside from the obvious subjective measures, like looking at an organization chart or naming a director or manager with that particular title, in practical terms several more precise quantitative measures would be appropriate.

The process for identifying measurement requirements—starting with the definition of stakeholders and proceeding to the production of a measurement plan and a set of measures (as described in Chapter 2) would be well applied here. The rest of the "measure" discussion will adhere to the principles outlined in *Project Measurement.*[1]

If you start with the stakeholders, what will ultimately manifest itself is the implementation of an improved project management capability for the organization. Senior management has both a high interest in the outcome of this project and a strong influence on how it will proceed. In defining the measurement associated with this project, management has three main purposes: (1) to ensure that the project provides an adequate capacity to provide the needed project management capability; (2) to ensure that the organization is defined with an adequate capacity to meet the current and future needs for this capability; and (3) to ensure that the quality of the services provided meets the organization's standards as defined by its six sigma improvement initiative.

Once the purposes of the measurement established to satisfy the information needs of senior management have been identified, we can focus on the metrics that will meet their needs. Measures of the capability of the project management organization can focus on two areas: (1) the qualifications of the people within the project management organization; and (2) the capability and coverage of the tools provided to the project management organization.

Since there are several forms of certification for project managers by both professional organizations and also internally by individual companies or organizations, it is appropriate to measure the attainment of these certifications as well as progress toward them. In keeping with the initiative to achieve six sigma levels of quality in project management, it is also appropriate to establish these certifications, their maintenance, and qualification beyond them as a measured aspect under this purpose.

In addition to certification, education in the field of project management and in the subject areas for the projects that will be managed is an appropriate measure that will indicate the capability of the project management organization. In this type of measure, the motivation value will be more useful than the actual results.

The final measure of the capability of the project management staff is experience, which can be determined based on the number and types of projects managed, as well as the amount of time spent managing these types of projects. In addition to the satisfaction of the measurement purpose stated by the senior executives, this is an example of a metric that could also be used by the project management office (PMO) to identify those project managers with particular types and amounts of project management experience as well as those in need of particular types of project management experience. The PMO is an assumed organizational entity responsible for organizing and managing the project management capability of the organization. Many organizations have these entities, which vary in the mix and scope of staff and line responsibility and authority.

After the staff capability is considered, it is important to consider the tools and tool support that are provided for use by the project management office. Since this illustrative organization is implementing the six sigma initiative for its own operations, it should develop and maintain a complete list of processes owned and managed by the project management organization. Using this information, the PMO will develop a deployment matrix that identifies the amount of capability, if any, that each tool provides for each process. As the experience metric provided a useful tool for levels of management below senior management, this metric will provide a considerable amount of information for facilitating the project management functions and assessing change opportunities in the evaluation or specification for new tools.

The next step is to develop an internal benchmark for evaluating the organization's current capability in each of these areas. Since individual departments currently have to provide their own project management capability, they would most certainly have some certified and experienced people and be aware of additional sources for such people, as well as possibly already have some tools and support capability in place. It will be important to consider how this capability is managed when the changes that are part of this project are implemented.

The next major area of purpose for the senior management metric is to measure and monitor the capacity and capacity requirements of the project management office. Here, it may make sense to talk about a benchmark measurement first. How much of the organization's resource use is currently and historically associated with projects? It will also be appropriate to measure "survey" data, where departments forecast future resource use requirements and also indicate current and future activity that is not specifically identified as completed under a project, but that may be more appropriately accomplished as a project.

The benchmark measures are a source of input for establishing the capacity objectives and goals for the project management office. Since the six sigma project for project management improvement is one and the same with implementation of the project management organization, these measures will help define the budget and the schedule for that project. As we discuss project management organization performance measures, we will see that these capacity measures and plans are also necessary for justification of the project management organization initiative.

For the senior management measurement initiative, the last area will focus on the performance of the project management organization. We have already noted that the six sigma standards will apply, which means that we must identify how we will measure the project management process. How will a defect be defined in the context of project management? How will an opportunity for a defect be defined?

One of the biggest challenges in this type of analysis is the need to separate project management from the projects being managed. You don't have to be an experienced project manager to have been exposed to the notion that project failures and project management failures are seldom distinguished from one another. Even more challenging is abandoning the notion that the success of a project is also a success of project management.

Project Management As a Process

It is imperative that project management be viewed as a process. As a process, it must have defined inputs, defined outputs, and activity that occurs in transforming those inputs into those outputs. As a formal process, it must have standards by which the inputs are evaluated and a means to reject insufficient inputs or to decide to go forward with insufficient inputs. As a process, it must have defined outputs and standards for those outputs. In addition, the process must define the alternatives for the outputs. With the processes and the standards defined, it then becomes more objective to evaluate the quality performance of the process.

If you look at process modeling and analysis, you will find, just as we did in researching the basics of six sigma, lots of manufacturing examples that analyze repetitive processes. Most of the tools available outline how to detail sequential steps and accommodate decisions, and the better ones even have the ability to define the performance statistics for each of the flows and steps. Some of these tools allow simulation of the performance. These probably share some similarities with the plans and deliverables you will be developing for the project being managed.

With your project, however, the plan is going to be executed once. The project process (plan) is developed after the alternatives have been considered and the one to be used has been selected. Moreover, the plan is scaled to the scope of the project for which it is being used. Contrast that with the project management process, where considerable flexibility and scalability are required.

For example, very small projects may not be able to tolerate the administrative overhead required to manage the average-size project, while a large project may well go out of control if the administrative activity is limited to what would be the right level for the average-size project. Also, with a stepwise defined process, many steps that are not necessary may be included. It is much more consistent with behavior in organizations to do something that is specified but unnecessary, as opposed to defending not doing something in a later analysis.

Similarly, some steps that are not part of a selected stepwise process definition may be necessary for managing a particular project. There is commonly as much reluctance to do something that is not required as there is not to do something that is required but not necessary.

The key to understanding non-repetitive process models is that while the steps and sequence are never the same from project to project, the means employed generally are the same. That is, in most cases, the same teams (individuals and skills) with the same management (individuals, styles, and leadership), using the same tools and techniques in the same environment will work on a different project. In any case, a myriad of factors (management, teams, tools, techniques, environment, etc.) can be measured in a way that relates the variation in these measures to variations in performance for any implementation.

Most project managers can cite examples of poor project managers who presided over very successful projects and probably some very good project managers where the project failed anyway (certainly all of my own projects!). Less clear is the notion of projects that were successful even though they failed to meet their budgets and/or schedule or even be accepted by their customers, as well as some successful projects that were canceled.

Remember, for the purposes of our implementation of six sigma in project management, the success or failure of the project by any construct is independent of the success or failure of its project management as defined in six sigma measurement. While there may be a strong correlation between the two aspects, for our purposes, it must be recognized that there is not a direct relationship between the two.

Another challenge that someone with even a little sense of the math might recognize is that measuring individual defects against opportunities presents a high risk of high fluctuation in the sigma level where there are very few opportunities for defects. Let's contrast project management with manufacturing.

In manufacturing, a process may produce millions of units in a short period of time; a project, however, can last several years. At least on its face, it would also appear that it is easy to identify a defect in a manufactured item: it either conforms or it does not. In project management, some of the output may be "wrong" because it is based on incomplete information or relies on assumptions that are known to be wrong. Of course, on the other side of that analysis, where it is easy to say that something that is not a defect really is one, it is just as easy to say that something that is a defect is not one.

For a discipline so deeply grounded in statistics as six sigma, what can you say for the validity of so soft a measure as the definition of a defect in a knowledge work product? Along the same lines, what can you say about a defect rate measured in parts per million where the apparent base is very few items?

As you define your processes and develop definitions for defects, establish the reporting cycles, and apply the metric across all the instances of the process during any reporting period, it is surprising how many opportunities for defects there are. As you begin the "improve" phase, it will also be surprising how well the measure tracks improvement.

The real focus of six sigma is not on the number of defects or the number of opportunities, or even on the sigma value (unless of course it is near six or better). The focus is on the process—improving it and maintaining the improvements. Developing an absolute intolerance for defects is far more important than developing methods to count them.

Metrics for Improving Project Management Processes

To review the senior management metrics identified:

Project management capability: Metrics about the qualifications of the project management staff and the tools and support provided for project management.

Project management capacity: Metrics about the number of projects and value of projects performed currently and in the past. Projections of the future number and value of projects are also included.

Project management performance: The sigma quality performance metric is the primary senior management performance measure for any process implementing six sigma process improvements. *Sigma performance levels are senior management-type metrics.* Anyone having the ability to actually influence the performance directly would have no real need to review this metric, nor would it be much help. The analogy of driving using only the rear view mirror fits perfectly.

Let's also look at the metrics requirements of the project managers and the project management team as they relate to the objective of improving project management processes. A complete list of processes was created to support executive reporting. In implementing the project management organization, these processes will ultimately be well documented and described and they will be available to support the management of projects. But these documents and tools describe only what should be done and at some level how to do it. Where deliverables are associated with a process, the documentation would also describe the criteria for the deliverable. What is probably missing is anything to define what is actually done.

In many accounting systems, project management is "overhead" or "administration." Certainly the individuals know what they did and have a good idea how much of each task type was done. They also know how each piece may be broken down in terms of creation, improvement, or rework, but this anecdotal information is wholly inadequate for achieving six sigma levels of performance. What is needed is an adequate "chart of accounts" or other cost collection instrument that will describe in accurate detail what is done and how much of each task type is done in the project management process.

While most of what is done in project management is viewed in terms of hours spent by the people involved, the cost collection mechanism also needs to capture dollar costs and provide a way to relate those dollar costs to other measures of cost. For example, say in one project, a contract scheduler is hired and the cost is shown as the amount of money spent on the contract. In another project, an internal scheduler is used and the cost is shown as the hours spent. For analysis, it would be necessary to capture the "cost" of the contract scheduler in the equivalent hours that would have been charged had an internal scheduler been used. An estimate would also be needed of the contract cost if a contract scheduler had been used instead of the internal scheduler.

This is where people and commitment issues arise as a major and ongoing challenge. Much project management work is "contingent," where the performer waits for something to happen before acting. A contextual example is the preparation of risk plans. Preparing the plans is "flow" or "stepwise process" work where the process continues until the plans are complete. For the most part, executing the plans requires the risk to manifest itself in some fashion; if it does not, then there is no action.

Of course, project managers and team members may be reluctant to record idle time as just that. Similarly, there may be times when managing a project involves a considerable amount of overtime with long days and maybe even work over holidays and weekends, but the project managers and team members may have concerns about noting actual time spent. To achieve six sigma performance, you have to have an objective view of process performance.

In addition to the view of project management activity facilitated by the chart of accounts approach, the project management team needs a metric or set of metrics for evaluating actual deliverables against any standards established for those deliverables. It is probably a natural reaction for most project teams to think this is already done as a matter of course, since in all well-managed projects the customer is an integral part of the process and approves many of the interim deliverables. But those project management work products are evaluated in the context of the project to which they apply. This new evaluation needs to be done wholly in the context of project management.

The method used in software development, the Fagan Inspection Method (see generally www.mfagan.com) is very effective for identifying defects within knowledge work processes and deliverables. In applying this approach to project management deliverables and results, independent inspectors are trained to examine the deliverables of the project according to the requirements set forth in the standards for those deliverables. The inspection requirements are substantially the definitions for opportunities for defects used in the sigma performance-level calculation, and the results of the inspections are the source of the defect experience data.

The inspection results of course support the decision to repair the individual defects found, but more importantly, they initiate the process that will fix the fault that introduced the defect into the deliverable in the first place. With the fault fixed (i.e., the process and standards updated) and with the revised standards used in subsequent inspections, the "lessons learned" process is automatically in place and any improvements are realized in future performance.

So let's review the operations-level metrics identified for the "measure" step of our project management organization six sigma project. First we develop the ability to track and classify all project management activity within the organization. This is done by using cost accounting principles to identify the labor hours and dollar cost (and their equivalents where appropriate). Next, we establish the means to evaluate all the project management deliverables by adopting an inspection methodology. This provides a substantial amount of both opportunity and defect data to support the performance evaluation and measures.

The last stakeholders we are going to analyze in the measure step are the tactical-level stakeholders, who are essentially managers over the project management organization. There are also other managers, like the mid-level managers over the various departments for which projects are being managed or where projects being managed affect their area of responsibility. We will not analyze their needs directly here, however, since they do not have an interest in separating the performance of project management from the performance of the projects within their areas of responsibility.

The metrics needs of this level of management are grounded more in the analysis of the data collected to support the senior management metrics and the project managers than in the definition of new metrics requirements that would identify a need for additional measurements from within the organization. For those at this level of responsibility for achieving six sigma performance levels within project management, sources of information that direct attention to possible improvements in the practice of project management are key.

At the outset, these sources are developed through internal benchmarking against the various project management practices within the organization to identify the baseline set of practices as project management is brought under one focus. Analysis and review of historical performance should help establish the baseline set of practices and definitions of the project management processes to be included in the process definitions. As the organization becomes proficient at executing these processes and as the project management is brought under control (statistically speaking), it is worthwhile to begin looking at innovations and improvements.

An in-control process (plus or minus 3 standard deviations, with no mean shift) is a long way from six sigma levels of performance. It is necessary to look outside the organization to identify what the best practices would be in your organization, culture, and with your current and anticipated project portfolio. Benchmarking is an excellent way to gauge your own practices and performance against others. If you can benchmark against the best, you can leverage your own improvements to the significant levels needed to attain six sigma levels of performance.

Another good approach for recognizing improvement opportunities in the practice of project management is by examining the various "maturity models" that have been developed for evaluating and improving the practice of project management. Doing the benchmarking and pursuing the maturity model improvement methods will reveal a great deal in common between six sigma and the many other methods that focus on collecting and organizing tools and techniques for understanding what you are doing, how well you are doing it, and how you can do it better. If there is a distinction between six sigma and the other methods, it is that instead of focusing on doing things better, six sigma focuses on doing things perfectly or as close to perfectly as possible.

The primary focus of the project management organization tactical metrics is on analysis of the data gathered to support the senior management metrics and the project management metrics. Key to that analysis is the development of an understanding of the context that determines the best possible performance and the ability to reach levels of performance that reach or exceed six sigma. This context is determined mostly through the comparative analysis possible via benchmarking against best practices or "right practices"—those that yield the best results in your culture and with your projects. Along the same lines as benchmarking as a context for identifying the right improvements is analysis of the various maturity measurement methods and concepts.

We have reviewed three key groups of stakeholders and identified their measurement needs and objectives as an illustration of a typical initiative to achieve six sigma in an organization where the starting point is ad hoc definitions of a project and the application of project management disciplines. It is important that the stakeholder analysis be carried out to completion and that all the stakeholders be identified and their measurement needs satisfied. The analogy is project management risk analysis. The risk that significantly influences the project is probably not one of the risks you recognized and planned for.

The DMAIC Process

Drawing an analogy between the DMAIC process and generally accepted project management processes, the DMAIC process is much like the initial planning steps of a project. The better those early steps are done, the easier the subsequent steps are and the less the risk of failure. The better we have defined the problems or goals and the measures that will guide us to the solutions to those problems or the attainment of those goals, the more likely the following steps will lead us to a success.

Like the warnings on the stunt shows on TV: these are professionals, don't try this at home. Make sure you have people with the right skills to analyze the data, and who are able to identify what the data are capable of telling you and also what the data are not capable of telling you—or, more likely, what they are not capable of telling you yet. Did I mention that the progress to six sigma is a journey? Don't be surprised that the analogy includes the chorus section in the back seat on the family journey: "Are we there yet?"

Knowledgeable and experienced analysts will not only be able to help you gauge your position and progress accurately, but will also be able to help with setting realistic expectations for results and progress. Arguably, many such initiatives fail not because they were not capable of meeting all the expectations associated with their adoption, but more because of unrealistic expectations of the level of commitment and the amount of time involved.

The next step is "improve." Project managers familiar with iterative or spiral-type development approaches will appreciate the concurrent nature of the DMAIC approach. In continuous improvement, there is the inherent notion of a continuous define-measure-analyze precedent activity, as well as a continuous control effort.

"Improve" really means change. Most organizations usually get the first part of change right but struggle with the second. The first part is that you must do something new or different from what you have done in the past. The second part is that you must discontinue doing something that you have done in the past or change the way it is done.

Nothing is sacred. Six sigma performance is very likely a dramatic change from your normal, albeit good, performance. Dramatic changes to results will most likely require significant changes to processes.

To achieve significant improvement you must identify what you are doing that you need to continue doing or do more of. You need to identify what you are doing that you need to change. You also need to identify what you are doing that you need to discontinue doing. And finally you need to identify what you are not doing that you need to do. If you scrutinize every-thing you do using the first three steps, your chances of success improve greatly. Many such initiatives fail not because they failed to do the right things, but because they failed to quit doing the wrong things.

For the same reasons you should call in the professionals to ensure that the measure steps are done properly, you need to call in the change management experts to ensure that the changes are implemented effectively. Again and again, I have observed how many people seem to think that because something was just changed, it is somehow foreclosed from being changed again. Consider our journey analogy: if we don't change our position continuously, we will never reach our destination.

The final step is "control." Project mangers should recognize that controlling change is much like managing risk. Ironically, controlling change is not like controlling projects at all. In controlling a project, each step is planned (and the plan includes the performance expectations of budget and schedule) and each step is done once. Each step in the change process is expected to be performed many times after the change. Each step will exhibit learning curve dynamics where initial performance may not be as good as the old methods for doing the same thing.

Moreover, the performance standards for a project are arbitrary. That is, the performance objective set for the project may or may not have any relationship to any standard for that particular item of performance. Contrast that with six sigma, which is an absolute standard of performance. If the change does not eventually result in improved sigma performance, then the change must be reversed or modified as necessary to improve the performance. Risk management deals with uncertainty, variability, and impact.

Any process change may or may not be an improvement. Any improvement from a change may or may not be evident in the first few iterations of the change, or in all instances of implementing the change. Controlling change involves the dichotomy of the error of reversing an effective process change too soon vs. the error of failing to reverse an ineffective process change until too late.

As you finally do achieve significant levels of performance, there will probably be some, if not considerable, pressure to reduce or eliminate some of the controls that are critical to maintaining the high levels of performance. Controlling how the stakeholders—who can influence the essential elements of maintaining six sigma levels of performance—exercise or restrain their control can be just as important as controlling processes.

Of course, if we must systematically abandon the past, we must consider that our DMAIC process is the systematic way in which we constantly improve on the way to achieving six sigma levels of performance. Going from "normal" levels of performance to six sigma levels of performance is not a superficial change. Characterizations such as "paradigm shift" or "organic change" or even "sea change" are apt descriptions of what you are undertaking. Issues relating to people and commitments will also arise and can pose great challenges. Simple theoretical solutions often have little relationship to the complex realities. On the other hand, great solutions to real problems can be achieved.

NOTE

1. Steve Neuendorf, *Project Measurement* (Vienna, VA: Management Concepts, Inc., 2002). © 2002, Management Concepts, Inc.

CHAPTER 8

Organizing for Six Sigma

Through most of this book we have assumed that the ability to implement a significant organizational change is not an obstacle to successfully implementing six sigma. Of course, the reality is that overcoming organizational inertia presents a significant challenge to making changes, even those that may mean survival of the organization in a changing environment.

Organizational change is a topic that has been studied extensively. Some major points are relevant to project managers involved in six sigma.

Maybe you have heard the expression "getting your ducks in a row." The etymology is not clear. I had always understood the expression to come from engineering, meaning getting organized to get things done. Back in the old days, it was common for engineering departments to be seemingly vast open spaces filled with drawing boards. Since most drawings were stored rolled up, it was not always easy to lay a drawing out flat to work on it and the drawing would generally have to be secured if it was to be worked on. The drawings were secured using specialized drawing weights that did not look unlike duck decoys. Especially when viewed across a vast expanse of green-topped drawing tables, the weights looked much like ducks on a pond. Disorganized engineers generally had their ducks scattered all over; when someone was well organized and ready to get something done, they had their "ducks in a row."

To continue with the metaphor of ducks in a row, there are five ducks: vision, skills, incentives, resources, and action. Once you get all five of your ducks in a row, change will happen.

VISION

If you get your birds mixed up, however, and instead of a duck for *vision*, you have an ostrich with its head in the sand, confusion results. A vision is a picture. What does the desired future look like? To be of any value, a vision must encompass goals; it must include a context that reflects the environment in which the vision will be a reality; it must be comprehensive to the point where it has valuable meaning to everyone who is expected to share a commitment to achieving the vision; and it must be controlling, where actions taken after the vision is articulated and accepted must be based on progressing toward achieving the vision—or they will not be undertaken.

The concept of "alignment" also applies. This concept includes alignment of the strategy and tactics of the organization with the vision. It also includes alignment of the various departments or subunits within the organization or part of the organization that is undergoing the change toward the common vision. Alignment also means that the individuals within the organization have common values consistent with a belief in and commitment to achieving the vision.

At the crux of the notion of alignment are the people issues that are often the predominant cause of failure of initiatives like the implementation of six sigma. Most activities and people tend to establish comfort zones, where they know what to expect and what to do. Anything that will disrupt activity and push things out of the comfort zone is viewed as "to be avoided." Project managers are adept at risk management, which is just that: keeping the project within the comfort zone described by the project plan. When something threatens, it matters that it is avoided—much more so than how it is avoided. If someone wants to offer a reason to explain why a particular change will not work, it matters more that the change is not attempted than it matters that the excuse was valid.

Consider a manufacturing example. Say that there is an initiative to improve one part of the manufacturing process that is producing 0.05% defective products. That might sound pretty good, but it is still only about 4.8 sigma. The excuse is that about 10% of the defects experienced by the customer are the result of post-production handling damage and other causes well outside the control of the manufacturing process. Even a significant improvement in the manufacturing quality will not have a measurable return on the investment in the improvements.

So maybe we should focus first on the handling and post-production. If we follow the "blame chain" clear through, we will find that all the significant problems occur beyond the doors of the factory. We would be wasting money to give them better things to break—right? It does not matter if this is right. It matters that we don't waste time and money trying to "fix" what is "not broken." The truth is that if the durability requirements were addressed adequately in the manufacturing process, the units would not be nearly so susceptible to damage from post-production handling and processes.

A project management example might involve the scheduling process. Why waste time and money trying to improve the scheduling process when the vast majority of your customers are totally inflexible about when they need their project delivered? The excuse works if nothing is done to improve the scheduling process, even though the reality is that if the scheduling process worked right, the customers could easily be brought to respect its results.

It may be apparent that both of these issues are process issues: first is the contention that the real problems are in another part of the process, and second is implying that the part of the process being improved is actually waste and therefore irrelevant. These are really people issues, with the intent being not to support the overall initiative and thereby to avoid changing the status quo.

Those offering the excuses are not "aligned." That is, they do not really believe in the initiative and are not committed to implementing it in their area of activity or all their processes.

Without vision, there is only confusion. Activity is not focused and can even work against other activity. Actually it is not really accurate to say there is not vision; rather, there is no common shared vision. Each individual and group will rally to spend the resources and reap the incentives, assuming that the other "ducks" are lined up. But with nothing in common to progress toward, there will be no progress.

SKILLS

If you get your birds mixed up, and instead of a duck for *skills*, you have a turkey (or a bunch of turkeys) without the skills needed to make the change and operate in the new environment, anxiety results. People without the skills needed to achieve and maintain the vision only become frustrated and afraid that their inadequate and inappropriate efforts will place them—and, assuming that they are committed to achieving the vision, the organization—in jeopardy.

Much of the criticism of six sigma as embodied in the current versions supported by the marketplace arises from its seemingly high costs. Many of those costs are associated with the training required of everyone in the organization and the extensive training required for the black belts, as well as the comparatively high costs of hiring or contracting people with those skills. On the other hand, without that knowledge and those skills, the risk of failure to achieve six sigma, or to gain any net improvements in quality, is very high.

People tend to assume that because they are good at what they do, they will be good at doing it differently. People also tend to assume that because they are good at what they do, they should be good at doing things related to what they do, like improving its quality, or measuring it, or managing projects that include what they do. The reality is that being able to do something well requires learning. Before the learning takes place, the performance is not nearly as good as possible and it is often inadequate to meet the objectives of the activity.

INCENTIVES

If you get your birds mixed up, and instead of a duck for *incentives*, you have an angry and obnoxious duck like the cartoon character Daffy Duck™, slow change results, if change happens at all. If there are negative incentives, at worst, sabotage will happen. Whether we admit it or not, everyone asks WIIFM ("what's in it for me?"). It does not have to be personal—the company may be a better place to work or may be more stable. Perhaps it is increased pride in the results. In formal six sigma, most of the successes are rewarded with significant and tangible rewards for the participants.

If the answers come up negative, such as recognizing that the improvement is realized by head count reduction, and yours is a head that appears to be at risk, or if the improvements will make your job boring or significantly different from what you have enjoyed up to the point of the change, then inertia will take over to make change slow and difficult.

Most change initiatives fail to appreciate the importance of the speed of change. Change can be too fast, and it often is because we tend to think of things in relatively short cycles. Many organizations that think they have been in business for, say, 20 years, have really been in business for one year, 20 times. Each year's results validates the decision to continue for one more year, and the business plan rarely extends beyond the next annual report. Budgets are often set for one year, with significant risk that items that are considered discretionary, like any change initiative, could lose their funding.

Consequently, change is usually "scheduled" to occur within one or a few consecutive budget events—sometimes years, but usually within a few quarters. Change is a process, just as managing a project is a process. There is a definite fixed time component to making a change as well as a precedence order that must be observed if the change is going to be successful. Trying to compress the fixed time or ignoring the precedence order will almost guarantee that whatever was hoped to be changed will revert to what it was before the change was attempted.

Conversely, if it is recognized that some change will take longer than the typical planning/funding cycle, there is usually a strong tendency to stretch it out further by putting higher priority items in front of it. Under these conditions, the change can lose its momentum and people will start to question the commitment to the change and to making it happen. No matter how strong the commitment to change, the likelihood that it will supersede the commitment to produce is small.

I still cringe at the managers who say that you cannot change a tire going at 60 mph, when from the outside it is clear that the tire that needs changing is smaller (or larger) than the others and they were going in a hopeless circle—or that they are going 60 mph when what is really needed is to be going mach 2. It is of utmost importance that the incentives reward progress toward the vision while they discourage failure to change—and it must be appreciated how great a challenge that can be.

RESOURCES

If you get your birds mixed up, and instead of a duck for *resources*, you have a welter weight of a bird like the cartoon canary Tweety Pie™, frustration results. In business and in organizations, everything costs something in time, money, and opportunity. Sometimes, initiatives fail because they had too many resources available, but more often it is because not enough resources were available. Not only is commitment demonstrated by sufficient resources being allocated and made available, but it is also shown through actions that manifest the belief that failing to make the change is not an alternative.

It is important to commit resources to make the change; however, it is also essential to stop the commitment of resources for whatever it is the change is supposed to supersede. Management must learn to "walk the talk" and make sure that what is done sends a clear signal that what was said is the real guiding principle.

For example, say that the changed process empowers the project manager to make certain decisions. If a department manager can get the project manager's decision overruled outside of the changed company procedure, say while golfing with the CEO, it becomes quite clear that by continuing to "provide resources" to the old political process the change was supposed to supersede, the CEO and the department manager are not really committed to the change.

ACTION

If you get your birds mixed up, and instead of a duck for *action*, you have a chicken, afraid to act, failure results. Just recently I had a valid occasion to use the expression "when all is said and done, there is lots more said than done." Just as it is said that time keeps everything from happening at once, in business and organizations, lack of time keeps anything from happening at all. Too often the organization will tell everyone that "achieving six sigma is a part of your job," but the reality is that everyone already has a full-time job with the time all filled up (and possibly then some). Everyone already operates with some version of quotas and goals and obligations; without clear direction about how those are all to be rearranged to accommodate the actions that will make the change happen, nothing much will happen.

Since I seem to be using a lot of clichés, it may be appropriate to close by saying that even if you have all your ducks in a row, and if it is apparent that they all walk like ducks and quack like ducks, it still does not hurt to take a close look to make sure they really are ducks. Your success as a project manager could depend on it.

Index

A

action, 65–66
ad hoc process, 27
airline safety example, 18
analyze step, six sigma, 30, 58

B

belts, 21–22
benchmarking, 43–44, 50, 56–57
best practices, 40
Bhote, Keki, 35
black belt, 21–22
bottom-up approach to data, 25
boundaryless collaboration, 28–29, 33
business process reengineering (BPR), 44
B versus C technique, design of experiment
   tool, 41

C

capacity, 29
certification, project managers, 49
component search technique, design of
   experiment tool, 41
conformance to specification, 15
control step, six sigma, 31, 59
corporate accountability, 48
cost, reducing, 16
cost of quality (COQ), 16
customer, focusing on, 24–25
customer relationship management (CRM),
   29
customized process, 27
cycle-time (T), 8, 16

D

data- and fact-driven management, 25, 32
defect add/remove rate, 17
defect density, 7, 23–24

defect rate formulas, 12
defect removal rate, 16
defects
   compared to failures, 8
   definition, 3
   opportunities for, 6
defects per million opportunities (DPMO),
   3–4, 11–12, 23–24
defect taxonomy, 7
define, measure, analyze, improve, and
   control (DMAIC)
   overview, 30–31
   project management, 48, 57–60
   purpose, 33–34
define step, six sigma, 30, 48
dependent variables, 8
design objectives, 2
design of experiment tool (DOE), 40
discovery rate, 16
DMAIC. See define, measure, analyze,
   improve, and control
DPMO. See defects per million opportunities
   for defects
drive for perfection, tolerance for failure,
   29–31, 33–34

E

effectiveness, 5
efficiency (E), 5, 8
executive metric, 25

F

fact-driven management. See data- and fact-
   driven management
Fagan Inspection Method, 55
failure
   compared to defect, 8
   consequences of, 16

fat manufacturing, 45
fitness for use, 15
focus on customer, 24–25, 31–32
full factorial technique, design of experiment
  tool, 41

G
goals, 15
green belt, 21–22
grouped data, 1

H
health, 5

I
improve step, six sigma, 31, 58
incentives, 64–65

L
lean manufacturing, 45
lessons learned, 55

M
managerial metrics, 25
martial arts terminology, 21–22
master black belt, 21
matrix management, 28
maturity models, 57
mean, 1, 10
mean shift, 23
measurement hierarchy, 25
measure step, six sigma, 30, 49–51, 56
median, 11
metrics, categories of, 5
mode, 11
Mount Everest Theory of Measurement, 26
multiple environment over stress testing
  (MOEST), 42
multi-vari technique, design of experiment
  tool, 41

N
next operation as customer (NOAC), 44
non-repetitive process models, 52
normal distribution, 11

O
operational metric, 8, 25
organic change, 28

output, 6
overhead, 54

P
paired comparisons technique, design of
  experiment tool, 41
parts per million (ppm), 10
passive data, 25
perfection, 26
performance standard, 2
plans, 26
PMO. See project management office
PMP. See project management professional
Poka-yoke, 44
positrol technique, design of experiment tool,
  41
ppm. See parts per million
precontrol technique, design of experiment
  tool, 41
proactive management, 27–28, 32–33
probability distribution, 1
process, 6, 9
process certification technique, design of
  experiment tool, 41
process focus on management and
  improvement, 25–27, 32
productivity, 8
product/process search technique, design of
  experiment tool, 41
project management
  capability, 53
  capacity, 54
  DMAIC process, 57–60
  measurement issues, 49–51
  metrics for improving, 53–57
  performance, 54
  process issues, 47–48
  viewing as a process, 51–53
project management office (PMO), 50
project management professional (PMP), 21
project measurement, 49–51
projects, 26

Q
QFD. See quality function deployment
quality
  improving, 15–16
  six sigma level of, 17–19
quality control, 16–17

quality function deployment (QFD), 42–43

R

resources, 65
response surface methodology (RSM) technique, design of experiment tool, 41
rework, cost of, 17

S

sandbagging, 29
scatter plot technique, design of experiment tool, 41
SCM. See supply chain management
sigma, 1, 10
sigma-level metrics, 10–13
skills, 63–64
SPC. See statistical process control
spec limit, 2
stakeholder analysis, 25, 56–57
standard deviation, 1, 10
statistical process control (SPC), 11
strategic-level metric, 8–10, 25
success, 26
supply chain management (SCM), 28–29, 45

T

T. See cycle-time
tactical-level metric, 8, 25, 57
tactical-level stakeholders, 56
total productive maintenance (TPM), 44
training, 19, 22

U

ultimate six sigma
    benchmarking, 43–44
    Bhote, Keki, 35
    business metrics, 36–37
    business process reengineering, 44
    critical success factors, 36
    customer loyalty metrics, 37
    design of experiments tool, 40–41
    mass customization, 42–43
    multiple environment over stress testing, 42
    next operation as customer, 44
    objectives, 35
    Poka-yoke, 44
    problem-solving method, 41–42
    quality function deployment, 42–43
    quality/reliability/cycle time metrics, 37
    self-assessment chart, 38–39
    success factor rating, 39
    supply chain engineering, 45
    total productive maintenance, 44
    total rating, 40
    total value engineering, 44
    21st century tools, 40
units of measure, 3

V

variables search technique, design of experiment tool, 41
vision, 61–63